The Revenge of Brand X

How to build a Big Time Brand™ on the web or anywhere else.

By Rob Frankel

MATT—
THIS SHOULD DO IT:
i'M THE "ONLY SOLUTION"
TO THEIR PROBLEM.

The Revenge of Brand X

How to build a Big Time Brand™ on the web or anywhere else.

By Rob Frankel

Printed in the United States of America
Library of Congress Cataloging-in-Publication Data
LOC# 00-132242
Frankel. Rob
The Revenge of Brand X: How to Build a Big Time Brand™ on the web or anywhere else / by Rob Frankel

ISBN:0-9679912-1-8

Disclaimer:

This book is designed to provide information in regard to the subject matter covered. It is sold with the understanding that the publisher and author are not rendering any professional services herein.

It is not the purpose of the publication to reprint all the information that is otherwise available to the author and/or publisher. You are urged to read all the available material, learn as much as possible from other sources to suit your individual needs.

Every effort has been made to make this publication as complete and as accurate as possible. But hey, we're human and there may be mistakes both typographical and in content. Therefore, this text should be used only as a general guide and not as an "ultimate source." Branding is as much a style issue as it is an art.

The purpose of this publication is to educate and entertain. The author and the publisher shall have neither liability nor responsibility to any person or entity with respect to any loss or damage caused, or alleged to be caused, directly or indirectly by the information contained in this book.

If you do not wish to be bound by the above, you may return this book to the publisher for a full refund.

*To Mom, Dad, Kim, Ricko, Android, the Booky
and of course, ALL the FrankelBees*

"Know thyself." — *Socrates*

"To thine own self be true." — *William Shakespeare*

"Don't be a schmuck." — *Rob Frankel*

The Revenge of Brand X

ACKNOWLEDGEMENTS

Well, isn't this a fine little place to begin a rant.

I'm not going to get all wet and sloppy about this, but I do have a bunch of people to thank for making *The Revenge of Brand X* possible.

Numero Uno on the list has to be Jaclyn Easton, friend, pal and author of the classic *StrikingItRich.com*, for her support, drive and cravings for lobsters. I can honestly say that if it weren't for Jaclyn, you'd be reading a Sidney Sheldon novel right now.

I want to acknowledge my mother, who now has something about which she can brag to all her friends with sons who have M.D.'s after their names. And let's not forget my father, for whom I wrote this book in the hopes that it would finally clarify what I actually do for a living.

I want to thank my wife for putting up with me. Not for anything having to do with the book, mind you, it's just that I can be a pain to live with. I don't want to thank my kids for anything, but it occurred to me that telling them how much I love them in print ought to score some points a few decades from now when they try to warehouse me in some old folks home.

Special mention -- in fact a whole paragraph -- goes to Don Parris, perhaps the last attorney in the world whose diligence, skills and energy are matched only by his generosity, wisdom and compassion.

Let's not forget those wonderfully supportive FrankelBees, whose energy and enthusiasm have inspired me to explore the human and business issues that made this endeavor so rewarding.

I'd like to thank the executives at Paramount Pictures for making this book into a feature length movie. I'd like to, but since they have no plans to do so, I'll skip them.

Finally, thank you for buying the book. If there's anything else I can do for you, let me know online at *robfrankel.com.* You'll know me. I'm the one with the obnoxious bobbing head.

INTRODUCTION:
THE MEDIA IMPLOSION

There's no question that branding is the most misunderstood concept in all of marketing. There are those who think of branding as nothing more than a logo. Others profess that branding is actually the positioning of a company's product or service in the public's mind. Both notions carry a certain amount of validity. It's true that people do need to recognize your brand (logo). And it's also true that people need to differentiate your business from those of your competitors. But while those may both be true enough, stopping at that point is most critical mistake that people make, for two reasons.

First — and most obvious — is that branding is much more than a simple tweaking of corporate identification. Although I devote whole chapters to this topic later in the book, let me just state at this point that a brand is much more than an identity, in the same way that you are much more than your name. You're a human being, unlike any other human being, with your own quirks, talents, scents and irritating habits. People may like you — or dislike you — for those attributes. But like you or not, you can rest assured that those people are not making their assessment of you on your name alone. More than likely, they're observing you, taking in all sorts of ancillary data about you as you move through their lives. How you speak. The words you choose. Your idea of fun. The way your eyes sparkle. Your idea of ethics. How you treat your dog. And the list goes on.

The point is that your brand is more than mere identification. But I'll get into all that much later. For now, let me address the reason why branding is more important now than it ever was before. It's the less obvious approach to branding, coming at you from a totally blind side of even the richest marketing guru in his finely pressed blue suit:

It's all about the media.

The end of media slavery: How branding is rooted in media

To really understand where branding is going, you have to understand why branding exists in the first place. And the reason why branding exists comes down to this:

Choice.

But not choice in the way traditional branding pundits would have you believe. Their old models stress the choice of products and services among competing factions. Which means that in their world, you choose between varying brands of shoes before deciding which pair you eventually slip on to your tootsies.

But that's not the choice I'm talking about.

The choice I'm referring to is your choice of media. That's what affects branding more than anything else, my friend, and now I'm going to tell you why. It may take a little while, but trust me, this is crucial to your understanding of branding if you intend to fully utilize its power. Besides, my publisher insists on longer chapters and word counts.

Ready? Here we go.

As far back as anyone can remember, the media has been controlled by few who in turn controlled the masses. In our modern society — say in the last hundred years or so — the term mass media began its notorious run with the advent of the newspaper. Thanks to the industrialized modern printing press, a couple of publishers determined which news your great-grandmothers and great-grandfathers read. Not only did those publishers decide on what they read, they also took on the task of deciding which items were the most important, which should be read first and which should be relegated to the pages in the way, way back.

It should also be noted that these very same self-appointed guardians of public information wielded enormous power of what great-grandma and great-grandpa did *not* read. The basic model became firmly established for years to come: one source — maybe two — of information to be consumed by a massive population over a specific geographic area. Until the early 1900's, if you needed to know about something, the daily newspaper was your primary information source. Sure, there were weeklies and monthly magazines, but they, too, followed the same basic model, offering millions of inquiring minds extremely few options.

The model became even more restrictive with the advent of news services, which reached beyond the realm of local reporters and became a central source of international and national news. The data flow narrowed even further, because theoretically, the entire newspaper-reading world could conceivably gobble down the wrongly-reported story of just one reporter and risk misinforming an entire nation.

Throughout the first half of the century, the model didn't change although technology did. Radio profoundly affected the rate of information transmission, if only to include the illiterate among the ranks of the fully-informed. But even radio stations were few in number compared to the total population, and to add insult to injury, they too often procured their news items from the very same newswires as the press.

By mid-century, television arrives on the scene — with little variation on the same theme. Although news organizations began to develop more sophistication, the sources for that news remained modeled on the same basic principle: lots of stories, reported by few and disseminated by even fewer media.

The lagging technology didn't help things, either. By mid-century, there were no truly national networks as we now know them. There were national affiliations of radio and television stations but they resembled something more along the lines of a farmer's co-op, sharing the efficiencies of buying programming and selling advertising space. The first satellite launch was still decades away, which meant that as recently as the 1960's, Mom and Dad were still being spoon-fed only that data which those few media would deign to dish out.

By the 1960's, however, technology began to catch up. Unfortunately.

I say "unfortunately" because while broadcast and satellite technology allowed the media to hook up and entire nation live — and eventually — in color, it also had the effect of streamlining information delivery even further. Now, only one source of information need be beamed out to as many TV, radio and newspaper stations as could pay for the privilege. Of course, by this time, properties in radio, newspaper and television had begun to consolidate into our modern day networks. In the age when "thinking big" was the rage, the networks did just that, wiring together as many media properties as possible, skirting the limits of Federal legislation defining just how much media one company could own in one market.

The effect is best illustrated by television, which by 1960, became dominated by three national networks: CBS, NBC and ABC. And anyone who remembers the 1960's and 1970's knows that if anything was happening on television during those decades, it was happening on network TV. Sure, there were small, one-lung, camped-on-the-edge-of town type local stations, but nobody ever took them seriously. And lobbyists struggled to keep a straight face when they argued the viability of UHF (Ultra-High Frequency stations that most televisions couldn't even receive without a special antenna) as competition for the networks. The fact is that if you were watching television, you were watching the big three. And this is why:

First, they owned a hugely disproportionate share of television stations. From 1960 forward, each of the three networks did what they could to buy up as many territories as they could. And what they couldn't buy, they tied up with affiliate agreements.

Second, the amalgamation of media channels led to a decrease in programming. Good news for the television industry, bad news for the rest of us, who flipped through three channels to find the same awful programming, no matter which city we lived in. The media got to cut programming costs and sell more advertising inventory. And even though it may have been fun to chatter with your cousin in New York about the last episode of *Gilligan's Island*, the truth of the matter is that both his and your viewing choices had been whittled down even further.

By the 1950's and certainly the 1960's, at least three generations had witnessed the progressive deterioration of their choices in information gathering. By this time, people growing up in America were actually thinking it normal to make their decisions based on what they saw on TV and heard on the radio. Major fortunes were created literally overnight, as manufacturers placed new products in front of families on Sunday night during commercial breaks on *Bonanza*. It got so bizarre, that even sociologists proclaimed early evenings as "the family hour", where American families ostensibly grew closer through their collective television viewing.

Think about that for a moment. Tens of millions of people, all watching the same program at the same time. Then think about those same people having maybe two alternatives to what they're currently watching. It gets pretty scary when you realize that for several generations, hundreds of millions of people's choices in media were restricted to a mere handful of options. The phrase become coined as "mass media" because anyone with enough money could literally reach the vast majority of the population with one effort. New products could go national overnight — and did.

In the late 1960's for example, women were just beginning to liberate themselves from their bras and girdles, often purloining their boyfriends' and husbands' clothing as the more comfortable alternative. It wasn't until a few years later that the first jeans "designed specifically for women" were introduced. The brand was called Dittos Jeans, whose point of difference was effectively illustrated in less than thirty seconds by a beautiful young girl in her twenties asking the audience if her blue jeans fit her well. They did, but not as well as when she took them off in front of the camera to reveal she was wearing Dittos jeans underneath the blue jeans.

You don't see that kind of effective commercial on television anymore. In fact, Dittos didn't have to run it very often, either. They ran the spot twice in one night on the same program — the nationally-broadcast America's Junior Miss Pageant — and owned a national brand the very next day.

Dittos exemplifies the effectiveness of mass media. It also demonstrates the power that demographics once enjoyed in the mass media age. Because there were so few media choices, it was easy to aggregate a huge audience. Mixing those few media choices with demographically-designed programming completed the process. In Dittos' case, it was amassing millions of teenage girls with a beauty pageant aimed at their tastes and interests. It couldn't fail. They had nowhere else to go. What would they tune to, *Gunsmoke*?

The Big Three dominated the television scene for another generation, honing their programming skills not on the tastes and wants of the American viewing public, but on their insatiable drive to accurately predict and deliver demographically consistent audiences. Demographics, for those of you unfamiliar with the term, is the practice of dumping people's characteristics into quantifiable categories and then basing your strategy on those numbers. It could be "white, male mental patients between the ages of 26 and 34." Or "female psychiatrists in the Detroit area over the age of 40." You get the idea. In any event, now you know why television shows are never created for their intellectual promise, but for their appeal to the widest audience, which when you think about it, makes the whole concept of the Emmy awards somewhat amusing.

But what, I hear you asking, does this have to do with branding?

Everything, my friend, and more.

How the web has reconstructed media models

The Mass Media model thrived well into the 1970's and even the 1980's, scoffing at any and all that attempted to dislodge its dominance. Even the introduction of cable television didn't phase the Big Three. In fact, cable television companies became a fashionable tax shelter scheme for a while.

But cable did manage to do the one thing that no other medium had managed to accomplish: it gained a foothold in the quest to open up alternative information channels to the viewing public. Cable's first attempts at original programming were truly laughable low production short features and public access diatribes by local nut cases. And it was these tiny little cracks in the monolithic media monopoly that heralded the Great Media Implosion. It began with a small number of American communities getting a taste of media freedom. As pathetic as they may have been, programs began appearing on odd-numbered channels, produced at very low cost by very ordinary people. People whose messages weren't at all relevant on both sides of town, let alone both coasts of the country.

By the 1980's America's infatuation with Public Access cable TV came of age with — ironically enough — its first national media exposure. Millions of viewers took up the cause, following in legions by the likes of *Saturday Night Live's* comic representation of *Wayne's World*, a recurring bit about two post-adolescent dopes who broadcast their Public Access show from their basement. The concept became so popular with the American public, that cable companies who previously couldn't give their public access time away suddenly found themselves swamped and over-booked. *Wayne's World* itself went on to spawn two feature-length movies.

Anyone who was paying attention could see that the American public liked the idea of taking back control of the media. And if you look closely enough, this is where we find the beginnings of the end of mass media. The end of four generations of media slavery.

In short, this is the point at which *mass media* becomes *media for the masses*.

I call this the Great Media Implosion because in just a few short years, one hundred years of media-dominated information crumbles from its monolithic proportions. Within those few years, the number of cable television stations soars. Satellite transmissions increase the availability of program content to anyone who can bolt a dish on to their roof — for thousands or dollars at first, for just a few hundred later. Television sets move from 70 channel cable-readiness to well over one hundred, with an increasing number of them niching into special formats. There are science channels and movie channels. And within the movie channel segments, there are special channels for niched movies: romance channels, classic channels, science fiction channels.

By the early 1990's there are television channels devoted specifically to food. Twenty four hours a day of omelet preparation, followed by a seven part series on the evolution of the avocado. Somewhere down the dial, programming that's not even entertaining appears: home-shopping. Within a year, there are two more. All of this is happening by 1994, way before most of the world even knows about the web.

And then it hits.

By 1995, the Big Three. already plenty concerned as they begin to feel their grip on the American consumer's mind slowly slipping away, begin to freak out as the web explodes onto the scene, gobbling up the population's mind share at an exponential rate. By 1996, the number of web users is doubling every three months with no signs of slowing. America Online, having registered about six million people just a few years earlier, hurtles into 1999 with something closer to 20 million.

For the first time in history, the masses don't have to settle for being herded like cattle through the same few media conduits. The technology is coming that allows the masses as many choices as there are individuals, created by individuals who are members of the masses themselves.

For the first time in history, the masses have a choice.

Why branding is such an important factor in that restructuring

When I talk about choice, I'm not talking about viewing one television station out of hundreds. I'm talking about one web site out of hundreds of millions. Each with its own content, available twenty four hours a day, every single day of the year. Most importantly, though, is that every single one of those sites is available for viewing at the precise instant each viewer wishes to view it. Which means unlike conventional programming, the web is the first medium that's convenient for its users. It starts when they need it to start. It ends when they need it to end.

To the chagrin of Big Media, there's far less compulsion in the increasingly hollow threat to "tune in or miss the television event of the week." Who cares? Why should they? The public wants choice. The web gives them that choice.

And that's the reason why branding on the web is so critical.

As the price of personal computers and web-reading devices continues to plummet, more people than ever are enjoying their freedom of choice. As more people enjoy that freedom, a new class of entrepreneurs is emerging, offering them even more choices. Being the great playing field leveler that it is, the web allows most of these new businesses the ability to appear at least as large as their more established competitors. The result means more competition in more segments.

At first blush, you might think that more competition translates into merely increasing your brand's differentiation. And that's exactly what 99.9% of the world's branding experts would tell you, as well.

But you'd be wrong. And the reason you'd be wrong is because you'd have failed to realize the importance of the great Media Implosion on branding.

The implosion's affect is what radically altered my own personal branding discipline, taking it from a matter of simple product differentiation up to a level of Big Time Branding. Because only Big Time Branding takes media into account as part of its strategy. Big Time Branding realizes that conventional branding — that which merely stresses an identity and its attributes — fails miserably once the few channels which funneled hordes of viewers no longer exist.

In other words, the days in which Big Media controlled the few images placed in front of the masses, along with the times and places where they could be viewed, are ending. Giant sponsors can less afford to pin their hopes on displaying their wares in front of millions on the hopes that one or two per cent will buy.

And the reason is choice.

Because the web is a user-driven medium, users decide what they want and when they want it. But implicit in that model is the fact that unlike traditional media users, web users go online seeking solutions to their problems. They rarely go on to be sold on goods and services they don't need or want. Yet all non-Big Time Brands still present themselves in a self-congratulatory way that ignores their prospect's wants and needs. And that's why so many traditional "brands" fail on the web.

A Big Time Brand, on the other hand, plays directly to the web audience, because, as stated by Frankel's Prime Directive:

"Branding is not about getting your prospects to choose you over your competition; it's about getting your prospects to see you as the only solution to their problem."

Sure, differentiation is important. But the key realization about branding on the web is that its users aren't a bunch of couch potatoes drooling in front of the tube. These are people intent on finding the very best solution for whatever it is they're seeking. Thus, if your brand and all that goes with it isn't portrayed as that solution, they're going to click away to the next guy's page that *Yahoo* or *AltaVista* listed for them when they first searched the category. Freedom that comes with greater choice is a wonderful, liberating thing — until you consider the fact that something like 80% of all web users never drill down past the first page of a site. That tells you your brand better speak to them fast and effectively. You better solve their problem — instead of beating your own glorious chest — and you better solve it *now*. Right up front. On the home page.

That's the genius of the Big Time Branding. That's the failing of traditional branding. And that's why I spent this entire chapter tracing the evolution of Big Time Branding to its media roots, instead of its marketing foster parents.

It really all comes down to this:

The old Unique Selling Proposition is dead. From here on out, it's the Unqiue *Buying* Proposition that matters.

How the playing field gets more level every day as a result

Once you understand that supplying solutions to user is what branding — and Big Time Branding in particular — is all about, you begin to see why the web is such a level playing field. If for no other reason, you know that most larger companies still don't understand the concept of Big Time Branding. Which means the sooner you implement your own Big Time Brand, the sooner you enjoy a higher success rate, because while they're spending their resources touting their wares and patting themselves on the back, you're presenting real-world solutions to real-world problems in real-time to real buyers.

That has even more implications than first meets the eye. Consider that since Big Time Branding focuses intently on providing solutions, the issue of presentation actually becomes moot. A prospect seeking a solution to his or her problem doesn't really care about how expensive a site is or how large the company looks. That prospect cares about one thing: how tuned in you are to his or her wants and needs.

All of which renders the whole concept of size completely obsolete.

So while P&G may spend 40 million dollars on a self-congratulatory site, they won't be selling a whole lot of anything to anyone real soon. In fact, pound for pound, the tiny entrepreneur who sells custom gift baskets of hand-made soaps will do way better, because she knows why people are coming to her site. She knows they're looking for what she produces. Amongst her competition, however, the winner will never be the prettiest or most comprehensive site. It will be the site with the Big Time Brand. The one that says, "I know what you're looking for and I've got it in your size."

No matter what this week's pundits tell you, the web is — and will always be — the great leveler on the field of business. No production budget can harm you. No price cut can bleed you, as long as you remember Frankel's First Law of Big Time Branding:

Branding is not about you. It's about them.

Weak, traditional brands will continue to rely on high mass media awareness, further weakening themselves by ignoring the wants and needs of individual prospects. Big Time Brands, on the other hand, will leverage new media technology and specifically promote their solutions to individuals' problems.

The stronger your brand, the better you'll do.

It's The Revenge of Brand X and that's where we're all headed, chief, whether you like it or not. The only question left is whether your brand will be strong enough to take it.

ACTION ITEMS — INTRODUCTION

1. Make a list of all the sources from which you get your information.

2. Now go back to that list and include the names of all the people, relatives, friends, consultants, over-the-fence gossipy neighbors and everyone else you left out in #1.

3. List the main information sources you relied on 20 years ago.

4. List the main information sources you rely on today.

5. List the first three places you'd go to find out more information about something you want — and be honest.

6. Write down the date of your last visit to the library.

7. Combine all the lists to see where your *real* flow of information comes from, as opposed to what media buyers and planners might sell you. This is where the brands live.

1

FRANKEL'S LAWS
OF BIG TIME BRANDING

How would you feel if I spent the rest of this book telling you how wonderful I am? I could, you know. I could tell you that I'm really smart and exceptionally talented. I'm probably the best at what I do, which is branding on and off the web. The brands I create work better and more efficiently than any other brand developer's.

I could rave about how much and fun I am at parties. How I can shoot under 100 on just about any golf course, too. Want to know where I went to college? My shoe size? How about we go over how many other people love me?

Getting sick yet? Turned off? Hey, *I'm* getting nauseous reading this stuff. Which is exactly the mistake that almost every business out there makes when it comes to branding.

All about me.

Nothing about you.

Pretty disgusting, isn't? Would you want to do business with a company that only trumpeted its magnificence to the world? Of course not. Yet that's what millions of companies do every day. Not just small companies, either. I'm talking about the big boys – Fortune 500 types in blue pin-striped suits, whose board members have wives named Marge and kids named Chip.

Branding is arguably the most misunderstood concept in marketing. Everyone says they know what it means, yet nobody can define it. The result is that there are a lot of hacks out there, spewing out theories about branding, few of which make any sense at all, most of which are utterly useless. And that's the reason why so many so-called brands are as weak and limp as they are today. In almost every case, you'll find that what most people pass off as brands are really nothing more than names propelled into high public awareness by huge media budgets.

Most branding neophytes – including the ones married to Marge – know so little about branding that they all stumble into the same mistake: they refuse to acknowledge Frankel's First Law of Branding, which clearly states:

Branding is not about you. Branding is about them.

Think about it. *You* know what your product is. *You* know what your company does. Let's face it, you're your product's biggest fan. If it were up to you, everyone would be buying your stuff. So you don't need an education as to why buying your product (or service) is the money move.

Given that, why would you ever develop a brand that appeals to *you*? The fact is that your end-users are the ones who have to be sold on your stuff. They're the ones that need to know why your widget is better than the next guy's. Yet that's exactly the goof that almost every business makes when they attempt to do their own branding.

That's why I wrote Frankel's First Law of Big Time Branding. Before you can brand anything successfully, you have to consider for whom you're branding. And in every single case, that means you're branding for the end-user's benefit, not yours.

Of course, the term *end user* means different things to different people. For retailers, it's consumers. For business-to-business, it's, well, other businesses. Overall, I submit to you that an end user is simply anyone you've nailed in the crosshairs of your marketing gun. Business to business. Trade groups. On intranets or extranets, the point is that brands are for end users. They're the ones that need convincing — not you.

If there's anything that I want you to take from this book, Frankel's First Law has to be it. But if there are *two* things, Frankel's Second Law of Branding has to be next:

If the branding is wrong, so is everything else.

So many people have so little understanding of what branding is and how it works that they simply skip right over it in order to get to the sexy stuff, like television commercials and overly-technical web sites. Forget it, Jim. Big mistake. Because if you don't have your branding chops down from the very first note, everything — and I mean everything — else that follows gets further off track. The first derailments are the actual brand names. Then come the marketing materials. Then the advertising.

Then the yelling and the firings.

In fact, having your brand strategically and creatively locked is positively the best method for hiring employees. All it takes is one trip around a well-branded operation for you to know whether a potential employee clicks in with your corporate ethos. Even more importantly, it tells you if he or she doesn't get it right away.

Hey, don't take my word for it. Flick on the TV. Or the radio. Or flip open the paper and pick an ad at random. See anything that means anything? Hear anything that makes a difference? Of course not. Because you can't build a solid marketing campaign without a strong foundation. The only foundation strong enough to support all that is a well-conceived, compelling brand.

A Big Time Brand.

When you start with a clearly articulated brand, you never have to worry about your television commercial delivering the wrong message. Your web site exudes the same tone and personality as the premiums you hand out at the national convention. Everything works together like a well-oiled machine, because every single gear in that machine is held to the same rigorous standards of that well-defined brand.

If it doesn't, it never makes it off the desktop — let alone out the door.

The challenge is understanding what branding is and how it really works before you can create one. And I'm not talking about something that your Aunt Doris thinks is cute or your kid thinks is cool. I'm talking about brands that drive stakes into people's hearts and leave them begging for more. The kind that get them to pay double retail and leave the store smiling.

You want to do TV commercials? Funny radio ads? Fine by me. Just make sure that your targets remember who the ad was for and why whatever you're selling fits *their* needs like no other.

That's what branding can do for you, Bob — if you know what you're doing. And that means getting the brand right before you do anything else.

Seven reasons to invest in a Big Time Brand

Before I get too far into the actual branding dance, however, I want to run down a few points that ought to really get your juices flowing about branding. After all, you've shelled out a couple of shekels for this book. It only seems right that you get a few benefits early on, if only to justify the item on your expense account. So let me start out by telling you some straight-to-the-bottom-line reasons why you want to march right into your boss's office and demand more attention be paid to your brand:

1 **Branding is the quickest return on your marketing investment:** This is one of my favorites, because I'm basically a pretty cheap guy. A strong, well-articulated brand provides the engine behind a far more effective marketing message, which means more people get your message right the *first* time. This means you spend less money on drilling the notion into their heads with costly media budgets. Lower customer acquisition costs mean higher profit margins, and higher margins are what get you the keys to the executive washroom.

2 **Increase customer loyalty.** Yes, it's true that we have all kinds of wires and screens to reach these people, but the fact of the matter is that despite the likes of modems, hard drives and fiber optic broadband, human beings are still far more emotional than we'd like to think. And for all your graphs and ledgers, more purchases are influenced by emotion – or at least non-rational — factors than anything else. Well-crafted emotion, I grant you, but emotion just the same. After all, there's a reason why the Porsche owner's manual is a thousand times thicker than a Hyundai's — you've got to justify a purchase like that with some semblance of rationality or everyone is likely to think you bought the car just to impress chicks.

As you'll see later on, emotion/non-rational factors play a huge part in branding. But for now, let's just say that while consumer loyalty has almost nothing to do with the left side of the human brain, it does account for still lower cost of sales through repeat purchases.

The fact is that people still prefer to do business with people they like. And nothing helps them justify their decision to return like a well-articulated brand.

3 **Raise end user frequency and response rates:** Think it's getting good? Take a gander at this: A well-crafted brand not only brings your end-users back for more, it also brings them back a whole lot more often. They come back because they like you. They come back because you like them and appreciate them. So you reward them and they reward you. Pretty soon you've built a mutual admiration society founded squarely on the attributes of your brand to the point at which your end users begin to feel a responsibility for your brand's welfare. When you find yourself in the middle of Brand Nirvana like that, you'll notice another convenient benefit: your end users not only visit more frequently, but they respond to your overtures more readily — at rates that average between 10% and 25%.

4 **Increase referral business:** Another advantage of a well-founded, well-articulated brand is that when people love you, they tell everyone else about you. No, let me re-state that: they *evangelize* for you. They get their friends, associates and grandmothers to visit more and buy more. You get third-party endorsements up the yin-yang, from satisfied end users who have personally benefited from, are incredibly excited about and loyal to your brand.

And you get them for *free*. Talk about lowering your customer acquisition costs!

Perhaps the best reason to hammer away at articulating your brand is that the more articulate you are, the more easily your brand can be integrated by your end user. And the easier it is for him or her to integrate it, the higher the likelihood of your empowering that end user to speak authoritatively on the subject.

Let's face it, The only thing people love more than being asked for advice is giving advice, and a well-articulated brand educates your end users so they can do just that. It's one of those non-rational things again, that is so universally consistent that you can set your watch by it.

5 **Increase market awareness:** Like a French avalanche, a Big Time Brand explodes out of the white noise of media clutter and gains momentum from there. Of course, not everyone who hears about your brand immediately races down to their local K-Mart to buy it. But the clarity and compelling aspects of a Big Time Brand sticks in the minds of those end users who clearly intend to buy sometime in the future. Which means that of its own accord, a well-built brand can not only help you increase your market awareness, but secure it, as well.

6 **Increase rates and profitability:** This is one of my favorites, mainly because it mirrors point #1 so symmetrically. I've already gone over how a solid brand can cut your marketing costs. Now you get to hear how branding can crank up your profitability.

When end users integrate a clear, concise and compelling brand into their consciousness, they move your brand away from its commodity status, into a place where price points suddenly don't matter. In fact, they're willing to pay a premium for your brand because they find it so compelling. Brand Valhalla. Every marketer's dream.

7 **Defend your market share:** Sooner or later, there are going to be times when the economy starts rotting. And when the paychecks start drying up, the first thing that poorly-branded businesses do is start cutting prices in order to preserve market share. It's embarrassing to watch grown men and women throw their products and service to the sharks like that, essentially wiping out the years of value they could have built for their brands.

In a bad market, panic rules the roost. I think Kipling put it best when he wrote something about the guy who stays calmest usually wins. In rough times, you'll find everyone panicking except for those who have invested in Big Time Brands. The reason they don't panic is because they know their products and services moved off from price points as a purchase criterion years ago

Because they're less sensitive to price than the other baying hyenas, the well-branded contingency gets through the cannibalism far more easily and emerges far more healthy than their price-cutting competitors.

Hey, didn't I tell you that this book was worth a few extra dinero? And I haven't even started yet. Give me another hundred pages or so and I'll have you swimming in silk.

Premium brand silk, of course.

ACTION ITEMS — CHAPTER ONE

1. Write down your company's brand strategy.

2. Now ask yourself why you're having such a tough time writing down your company's brand strategy.

3. Ask anyone in your company if they even *have* a brand strategy (mission statements are not brand strategies). If you finally get one, go to step 5. If not, go to step 6.

4. Try creating a company brand strategy.

5. Try creating a brand strategy for one of your competitors. If you have an easier time of it, it's likely due to the fact that you're an outsider, which makes the job a lot easier.

6. Create a "While You Were Out" message pad especially appropriate for your company's brand.

7. Look at the brand strategy you create and see if it can be found in every aspect of your company. If it can't, the company is not branded.

2.

WHAT, EXACTLY, IS
A BRAND, ANYWAY?

B efore we move too far down the road here, I should probably address the fact that almost nobody in America seems to truly understand what a brand actually is.

Well, that may be a bit harsh. Let me re-state that:

Almost no *branding expert* in America seems to know what a brand actually is.

Yes, that's much better.

Branding is definitely the most misapplied term in all of marketing. Like pornography, everyone seems to think they know what it is but still can't define it. So let me take a moment here and set our definitions straight. I want to go through a couple of examples that at most, should provide a common ground as to what branding is — and isn't.

The first example is a multiple choice test. It was going to be an essay, but my publisher refused to devote that many blank pages to the effort. This is a simple test to see how you might define what branding is.

Q: What is branding?

1 That thing they burn into cows
2. A logo or a trademark
3. A jingle or a slogan
4. I don't really know, but I'll look like a complete idiot if I admit it.

If you haven't guessed by now, the most popular answer — the one you'll find in most boardrooms — is #4. I can't tell you how many times I've sat in meetings with real life MBA's who sit on their hands or ask to refill your coffee when they're put to this test.

The actual answer is #1, "that thing they burn into cows." And it makes a whole lot of sense. The term "brand" refers to searing the hide of one rancher's cattle with his distinctive mark so that it couldn't be confused with anyone else's. You can't really blame him, either. After all, if you'd spent a lot of years in the cold, snowy plains driving smelly bovine across thousands of miles of prairie, you'd want to make sure you were getting top dollar for your steers, too.

The point, of course, is that if you work hard to mark your product or service that much better than everyone else's, you certainly want to make sure that the differentiation isn't lost on your prospective buyers. In fact, you want to go out of your way to make sure they don't miss it. In the rancher's case, that means burning the brand into the hide.

But branding goes far beyond the marketplace. Brands have been engrained in our lives for thousands of years. You just never thought of them that way. Want proof? How about this?

Hmmm. Pretty simple logo with fairly high awareness, wouldn't you say? And talk about emotional value. One look at this logo tells you all you need to know about it. It instantly communicates a lot about the person wearing it, too. Their principles. Their ideals. And on some music video channels, even what they're rebelling against. Very well-positioned. Extremely clear in its purpose. While it has had the advantage of several centuries in the market-place, I'd have to say that this one has all the qualities of a true brand.

So then, what are those qualities? What is branding?

Well, I'd have to start with the notion that branding is indeed about differentiation. Making it easy for people to tell you apart from the next guy that's trying to pry into their wallets. But it's more than that. Much more.

Branding in the Fourth Dimension

I get about half of my business through the web, which is just fine by me. Nothing enables my agoraphobia quite like moneymaking opportunities plopping themselves down on my desktop via e-mail. A number of inquiries are notes about someone's business, how it's beginning to grow and how they agree that establishing their brand is absolutely critical to long term, sustainable growth.

And then comes the Question of Doom:

"So, um, how much does a logo cost?"

Yeesh. This is where I begin to feel like Klaatu, the alien robot from another dimension, who freaks out the entire planet in The Day The Earth Stood Still. For those of you missed the movie, Klaatu pretty much blows our minds by doing weird things like making gasoline out of strawberries, or something like that. In any case, it's Klaatu's fourth-dimensional perspective on things that eventually inspire Earth's citizens' awe and admiration.

Then, of course, the air force tries to blow him up.

Nevertheless, I often have to take up Klaatu's mantle in order to explain that real, honest-to-goodness brands — brands with big muscles and plenty of hair on their backs - don't restrict themselves to one-dimensional stuff like logos and letterhead. They're intelligent life forms from the Fourth Dimension that can transform your business at warp speed.

Branding in the First Dimension tells people *who you are*. Its most basic species can be spotted as a full color corporate symbol napping gently in the middle of your business card. Perhaps a beautiful photo-rendering of Zippy the Gearhead proudly proclaiming, "Spacely Sprockets." That's fine. But just as with your favorite supermodel, looks alone will only take you so far. They may identify who you are, but not much else.

Branding in the Second Dimension tells people *what you do*. Sure, we know from Zippy's posture that your company is called Spacely Sprockets, but what about the other stuff you make? The Anti-Matter gasket seals? The Dilithium Crystal-based lubricants? A real brand communicates all aspects of your business, so that when faithful gasket-seal buyers venture into the lubricant market, they seek out your brand first.

Branding's Third Dimension communicates *how you do what you do*. The best down-to-earth example I can think of this late at night is an oil change. You know what you get when you take your Hyundai in for an oil change? New oil. You know what you get when you take your Mercedes in for an oil change? New oil and a beautifully washed car. True, you pay more, but you leave with more: the distinct impression that Mercedes takes real pride in the work they do. Which reassures Mercedes owners that their car purchase was a good one - and that their next one is a no-brainer.

Finally, we get to the Fourth Dimension, my personal favorite, where the gravitational pull of market forces stretch and shape your brand, producing a relevance your prospects find intriguing. It can be a quality claim. A product attribute. But whatever you choose, it has to be memorable, compelling and powerful enough to grab your prospects by the lapels, lift them off the floor and tell them they'd be complete dolts for choosing anyone other than you for whatever it is you're selling.

And if it's really killer, it can make us like you while you're doing it.

Federal Express did that by showing us that they knew the tortures we endure when our packages don't arrive on time. And they spoke to us in a way nobody else did.

I can hear many of you asking, "Gee, Rob, is there a Fifth Dimension?" The answer is yes, but they never had a hit after *Up, Up and Away.*

Frankel's Prime Directive

Okay, so now at least if you can't define what a brand is, you know what qualities a killer brand has to possess. And while the definition of a brand may be hard to articulate, my personal definition of branding reads as Frankel's Prime Directive:

Branding is not about getting your targets to choose you over your competition. Branding is about getting your prospects to see you as the only solution to their problem.

Gives you chills, doesn't it? I know. Me too.

If you look closely, you'll find traces of Frankel's First Law of Branding there. The one that states, "Branding is not about you. Branding is about them." Remember? This is a critical point that separates the real brands from the blowhards. This is the bell you want to ring in your end users' heads when they give you the once over. You want them to see your competition and come running your way

41

bellowing, "Nobody understands me the way you do!"

That's what gets them in the door — and keeps them coming back for more.

Once you've developed that Fourth Dimension brand, Frankel's Second Law kicks into gear. Remember that one? How if the branding is wrong, everything else is too? Now you know why that's so important. Imagine making as powerful a promise to your end users and then ignoring it in every other piece of communication that your company sends out. Instead of clear, compelling communication, you'd have chaos in a major key.

How to tell a good brand from a bad one

Because brands are so much a part of the social fabric these days, it's pretty important to accept the fact that so much of what branding is, is rooted in that social fabric. What that means is that Big Time Brands leverage off those cultural aspects, integrating them in along with all the other stuff you find traditional marketing books.

For example, *differentiation* is a traditional concept. But differentiation from a simple *strategic* point of view doesn't cut it any more, mainly because the lawyer-driven dynamics of the mass-communications world has forsaken clarity for "what the fewest people will object to." The result, as I'll show you a bit later, is a whole lot of something that usually means nothing.

So how can you tell a good brand from a bad one? Pretty simple, really:

1 **Delivers the message clearly:** I don't know if it's our university system, but someone out there is teaching people that if you just use enough syllables, you'll eventually impress — or bore — your audience enough to the point that they really won't care about what you're saying.

Alternatively, our politically correct culture dictates that taking a stand on just about anything guarantees that somebody, somewhere will take offense to it, spawning an entire industry that specializes in saying nothing with as many words as possible.

The best brands go against the cultural grain and make clear, concise statements. You don't have to be a creative genius to make these kinds of statements, either. Having contempt for lawyers certainly helps. But in any event, *simply stating something clearly* in a society weaned on weak generalities is the first step toward standing out from the crowd and creating a solid brand.

2 **Communicates quickly:** The same people who brought you multi-syllabic gibberish are also responsible for creating the short attention span. The bad news, incidentally, is that attention spans aren't getting longer, either. In the age of the quick cut music video, where scenes seldom last more than a fraction of a second, an entire generation has grown up to believe that if they don't dig it in a second, it's time to change the channel. This has never been truer than it is on the web, where your home page does it all. If your brand doesn't get them the second after they've hit you, they're back to the search engine's listing of everyone else in your category — and you're dust.

3 **Projects credibility:** Sometimes it seems that everyone's been trying to sell me something since the day I was born. I don't mind that so much, except that somewhere along the way, their claims, language and promises became so ridiculously inflated that they actually mutated from non-believable all the way to becoming laughable.

A few pages or chapters from here, I'll go into that with you more deeply.

If I forget, remind me.

4 **Strikes an emotional chord:**   No matter where I travel or who I meet, the reaction is always the same: everyone concentrates on technology, products — everything but the people who do the purchasing. Even on the web, programmers push pounds of technology across the wires, promoting its efficiency while forgetting that technology ain't doing the buying.

The technology is there for one reason: to put people in touch with other people.

It's the same thing with a Big Time Brand . It's not about you. It's not about your product. It's not about your service. It's about *them*. It's about *their* problems and *their* solutions. And that's an emotional contact. Sure, it's driven by your strategic goals and objectives. But it's the brand's job to integrate the two of them to the point where they become inextricably intertwined.

A Big Time Brand makes it easy for people to *like* doing business with you. And believe me, that counts.

5 **Motivates the respondent:** When people like doing business with you, they're more prone to actually doing business with you. But lowering that barrier to sales does nothing for you unless to close that sale. A Big Time Brand will motivate the respondent to cross that line.

It could manifest itself as a higher rate of response. Or higher purchase per visit. Or greater propensity toward upsells. In any case, a Big Time Brand not only presents its solutions, it draws in end users to try it, as well.

6 **Creates a strong user loyalty:** Out of all them, this is the one for which branding is most widely known. Yet it's just as misunderstood as the rest because it's almost always wrongly attributed to any number of causes. The very best brands are a mix of rational differentiation and compelling personality. Two powerful ingredients that cause end users to invest their emotions/non-rational feelings — along with their wallets — into your brand.

All of which brings us to Frankel's Third Law of Branding:

Advertising grabs their minds. Branding gets their hearts.

First you create the brand, *then* you raise the awareness of the brand. As you can see, doing it the other way around makes absolutely no sense at all, yet that's exactly what most of mainstream America does every day of the year.

Bad news for them. Good news for you.

ACTION ITEMS — CHAPTER TWO

1. Write down every attribute your company offers or sells.

2. Rewrite each one so that you're not selling it, but describing how it will help someone.

3. If someone gave you that list, would you thank them for being helpful? Or hate them for trying to sell you something?

4. Add three products or services based on that list that you can give away for free.

5. Construct a method of distribution so that you *can* give it away for free.

3.

BIGGER THAN BOTH OF US —
AND STUPIDER, TOO.

Okay, so here we have this Rob Frankel guy and all he seems able to do is preach this and harp on that, right? Wrong. Before I finish this chapter, I'm going to accomplish two things. The first thing I'm going to show you exactly what a brand can be if you let it. The second thing I'm going to show you is how the biggest, richest and supposedly brand-savvy companies on the planet have less idea of what good branding is than you or I do.

Yes, it's time for another branding test.

This time, I'm going to put you into two different situations in order to experience two different brands. I want you to put yourself in an end-user's shoes. I want you to close your eyes and imagine yourself as an end-user who has a real problem on his hands. I mean big trouble. Then I want you to select the brand you feel will solve your particular problem the best. Ready? Here we go:

Situation #1 finds you waking up in a small room. A very small room. It's wet and kind of smelly. The walls are covered with graffiti. There are no windows and where a front door should be are a row of cold, rolled bars of steel. To make matters worse, the gentleman standing outside your suite speaks only one dialect of some strange language, is constantly stroking his semi-automatic weapon and occasionally, leering at you with a more-than-amorous gaze.

You, my friend, are in a foreign jail. No passport. No identification. No money. And the only entertainment for miles around is the betting on which of the guard's teeth will likely drop out next. You are, as the saying goes, in deep yogurt. Quick — which brand do you want to see solve your problem?

Smith & Wesson?

American Express?

Think about it for a moment. Then, when you have a clear logo in mind, turn the page.

There you go. Isn't this the brand you want solving your problem? The old stars and stripes? Old Glory? John Wayne? Of course it is. This is the logo you want riveted to the lapel of the suit of the guy with the well-combed hair and the no-nonsense attitude who boldly strides into the prison, marches up to your cell and utters, "Henderson. State Department. We'll have you out of here in no time."

Right?

Think about how you feel in that situation. One moment, all alone and helpless in a distant land. Next moment, rescued by the very essence of Freedom, Liberty and everything else for which it stands. If you've ever traveled abroad for an extended period of time, you've had the same experience. You can't wait to get back home to baseball and hot dogs and apple pie. Even the Florida Marlins start looking good.

That mix of rationality and emotion is what great branding is all about. In an instant, you know what's coming down the road when you wave the American flag.

Now let's check out another example of branding.

This time, you're an end-user with a problem, only the problem you're having is that the report you swore you'd have on your boss's desk by tomorrow morning has little if any chance of arriving there on time — if at all. While you torture yourself for downing that last extra beer with the boys, rationalizing that all the report really needed was a few final touches, it now appears all too obvious that the touches it needs are actually major rewrites. It's two o'clock in the morning. You're clacking out as much data as your nicotine-stained fingers can possibly deliver when all of a sudden, your machine crashes.

You are in *dire* need of tech support.

Visions of yourself standing on the street corner bearing a sandwich board stating "Will analyze demo-graphics for food" swirl through your head. You begin to panic, knowing that if you don't get through to tech support, there is no point in going home to a spouse who's already waiting at home for you with a monogrammed rolling pin.

Again, you're in a seriously bad situation. Turn the page and ask yourself if you get the same feelings from this brand:

Microsoft

Hmmm. Not quite the same feeling, is it?

Yet here it is, arguably one of the major economic forces on the planet and it doesn't exactly make your heart swell with, well, anything. What you've got here is a pretty convincing demonstration of just how good — or bad — a brand can be. One communicates everything instantaneously, fusing its rational assets with an emotional zap. The other is....big.

What I'm here to tell you is that great brands go way beyond whatever it is you have to sell. Great brands motivate. Compel. Inspire. And there's absolutely no reason why yours can't motivate, compel and inspire, either.

Another point I hope this illustrates is that for the most part, the bigger they are, well, the bigger their mistakes are. Size has nothing whatsoever to do with how good or bad a brand is. Want more proof? Watch this:

Next time you're in the market for a new car — preferably an American model — ask yourself this: does it really matter if it's a Ford or a Dodge? I've got to tell you, to most people, it makes no difference at all. In fact, one of my favorite stories concerns my lovely bride who went to buy a little black pick up truck. She had decided on one of those little black Dodge light utility vehicles — and came home with a Buick "Jimmy". That would have been fine, except that she mistook the Buick dealership for the Dodge. Talk about indistinguishable brand differences.

Coca-Cola s another biggie that is terribly branded. Sure, they own a global share of market. Yes, they've been a great stock to own. But a great brand? Not by a long shot. After all, if you stroll into the diner and the waitress tells you they only serve Pepsi, are you *not* going to order it? Are you that loyal to Coke that you'd stomp out of the diner, driven by your loyalty? I doubt it. Coca-Cola is a big brand. It's a successful brand. But when you get up close and personal, it's actually a very weak brand, which is why it keeps buying up rivals instead of competing with them.

Nike is another brand that people are somehow confused by. A great brand? I don't think so. Let's face it, if you walk into the shoe store and a comparable set of Reeboks are on sale for half the price, are you telling me you're not going to buy the Reeboks? Of course you will. And so will the rest of America because there's no compelling reason to cough up the extra bucks for the Nikes.

I could go on, but you get the point — I hope. Which brings us to Frankel's First Law of Media Hype:

Just because you've heard about it
doesn't mean it's well-branded.
Branding and awareness are not the same thing.

Unfortunately, we live in a media-driven world where businesses now have enough money to buy their way into our consciousness. When your existence is wall-papered with sponsored messages, it's easy to for lazy end-users to slip into a purchase based on their familiarity with a brand.

And if you have limitless budgets, I suppose you can keep buying that familiarity with all kinds of media hype and borrowed interest. Slap a celebrity on your product and you likely to send sales through the roof.

For a while.

The big problem with all of the cases outlined above is that every single one of them is dead in the water the minute anyone with a bigger budget comes along. Media is easy to buy and always sold to the highest bidder. So if your branding strategy is based on a flimsy premise of awareness, you're skating on paper thin ice.

First you build the brand. Then you raise its awareness, through public relations, advertising, promotions or anything else you can convince their investors is a prudent course of action. But like I said before, if the branding is wrong, so is everything else. And in these cases, there's absolutely nothing for any end user to hang on to. No cultivated loyalty. Just habit. And habits die as quickly as new fads are born.

Lest you think I dump on big brands for pleasure, I should give fair mention to some big brands that have gotten it right straight from the get-go:

Even though it's technically not a business enterprise, we've already seen how the United States of America has one of the strongest brands in history. The truth is that USA is how the world defines freedom in every sense of the word. Yes, the French hate us and Japan fought us in World War Two, but it only takes a few years and a couple of liberating engagements before both of them are lining up at their very own Disney parks waiting to get their pictures taken with Mickey Mouse.

While it's true that I am a diehard Macintosh fan, it has absolutely no bearing on the fact that Apple has been — and continues to be — a terrific example of branding. Every few years, as market experts predict its demise, Apple commands the loyalty of its hardcore followers. But don't take my word for it. Just try converting a Mac guy to Windows and see how far you get. At this very moment, millions of Mac users are furiously linking their machines into their LANs and WANs, determined to keep their workstation pure and free of PC's. Does it make rational sense? Not really. Is it branding in action? You betcha.

Now consider the opposite situation: you think it's so tough to switch a Windows user to a Mac? Hardly. Oh, they may whine a little bit, but you'll see none of the flaming passions or personal body blocks that you get from Mac users.

Further proof of Apple's brand strength is that it continues to grow/maintain its market share in an expanding PC market. Why? Because Apple gives it Macintosh users real solutions with real, meaningful differences. Forget the fact that among those differences is the opportunity to spit in Bill Gates' face. On second thought, don't forget that. It probably does figure into the emotional side of the equation.

Which really points out the weakness in brands that rely on high-awareness. Talk to Microsoft users and you'll find that most of them have no real allegiance to the brand. They use it because everyone else does. Or because it was a cheaper solution at the time. Absolutely nobody will jump up and exclaim the virtues of Microsoft products — most of which are pretty good. But that's my point. Even Microsoft fans will admit that Microsoft stuff isn't great, but it's good enough. All of which indicates that the day someone else develops a totally transparent, Microsoft-compatible replacement, the monolithic menace is in trouble. Real trouble.

Shaking your head? Hmmm, can you say *Linux*?

Still another favorite brand is Federal Express, whose brand promise of overnight delivery is as strong today as it was when it was first launched decades ago. No matter what your age or demographic breakdown, I'm willing to bet that the first overnight delivery service you think of is Federal

Express and not because they've bought your awareness. The proof of that is that you probably think of calling UPS for delivering your packages. But Federal Express owns the overnight delivery niche, and the emotional benefits that go with it. Face it, you have your choice of who knows how many overnight delivery services, but in all honesty, don't you feel a tad better when you hand off the envelope to a FedEx guy?

I sure do.

So where does that leave you? Hopefully with the idea that just because they're bigger, doesn't mean they're smarter. It's just that they have the bucks to spend to make it appear as if they know what they're doing. The reality is that brand strength isn't a function of media dollars; it's a function of branding brains. It's the realization that branding is the delicate balance of marketing strategy with human emotion. And it's your commitment to your brand that will ultimately determine your success.

As the world of mass media continues to decompose, the importance of niche marketing continues to grow. The more you niche, the more you succeed. And to succeed in those niches, you don't need a lot of muscle, you need a brand that communicates itself as the only solution to your end users problems.

You don't have to be rich to understand that. Just smart.

ACTION ITEMS — CHAPTER THREE

1. Make list of five brands you think are great.

2, Make a list of their competitors. If you can, grab the ads of each business and arrange them side by side.

3. Cover the logos in each ad. Can you tell which ones are which?

4. Take any of the major brands you selected and put it through the same steps you completed in Action Items — Chapter Two.

5. Reassess your initial feelings about bigger being better.

4

DOWN TO THE BOTTOM LINE

Well, here we are. I don't know about you, but I can't stand those books that really have only one thing to say and take about 300 pages to say it. That's why I'm going to give you the most important part of the book right here. Ready?

Branding is the most important thing you can do to increase your bottom line.

That's it. You can close the book right now if you want. But I wouldn't recommend it, for a couple of reasons. First, branding can affect your business so drastically that it's worth spending a little time and a few bucks to ensure your success.

Second, even though it's they key to making your business happen, there's more — especially online — to business than branding, and if you shut the book now, you're going to miss them all.

Finally, nothing pisses off the guy at the front counter of the bookstore (assuming you didn't buy a download PDF copy) more than a dawdler who bends back the front covers of books and then replaces them on the shelf. So why not take the book home, settle in for the night and let me fill you in on why branding is so important and how — if done properly — your brand can catapult your business into the stratosphere.

Before we get too far into it, however, let me just point out that branding works almost anywhere. On television. On radio. Online. You name it. A well-executed brand cranks your business by reaching through your prospects' senses and yanking their brainstems until they finally realize that nobody else in the known universe can possibly help them solve their problem better than you can. What you may not have realized, however, is that a well-articulated brand works where it counts the most: right down there on the bottom line. And here's how it does that:

The Bottom Line

When people can articulate their purchase decision — and I mean really get down into the details of why they made their decision to buy your brand — they actually become evangelists for your brand. They'll go on and on about why yours is better and how smart a decision theirs was. But if they *can't* explain your brand, they won't talk about it to anyone. And if they can't explain it, it's because *you didn't explain it to them.*

By articulating why they should buy your brand, you arm your prospects with ammunition to march into the boss and say, "We've got to have Brand X. No other widget will do, because Brand X gives us...." whatever it is you give them. The point is that the more you empower people to buy your brand -- the more reasion you give them to buy it -- the more likely they are to buy it — especially when most other yutzes don't bother to articulate what *their* brands are.

When people can articulate their decision, they tell more potential buyers about your brand, because it's easier to remember. A well-articulated brand — especially one presented as a solution to a prospect's problem — is going to have way more memorability than some chest-beating slogan that barely made it out of the focus group research.

You'll also find that, human nature being what it is, a brand that's more memorable tends to make the prospect fell more knowledgeable. And as long as there are egos, that's an aspect of branding that will never go away. Which means when you empower your prospect with a well-articulated brand that he or she can talk up at the health club to other potential prospects, those prospects are likely to be impressed enough to sear your brand into their memories for their next purchase.

I've always liked that part of branding, incidentally. There's nothing like empowering people with truth. I mean, here's a total win-win situation, in which by simply making your message clear in a compelling fashion, you're actually making heroes out of everyday people who could use a helping hand. Men who otherwise have no excuse for buying *Propecia* other than decreasing their bald spots suddenly get to expound on stuff like the virtues of its positive effects on their prostate glands. Neat. eh? And more potential prospects mean higher market awareness and higher propensity for future sales. *Ka-ching!*

When people can articulate how your brand is different, they invest their loyalty in that brand. That means they make an emotional (or non-rational) commitment to your brand. And as we all know, the toughest things to scrape off your shoe are emotional commitments.

Face it, if you're told in a rational manner that something is better for you, you *might* make the change. But when the same data is presented to you with an emotional spin, the average human being moves much faster. Want an example? How's this: both Federal Express and the United States Postal Service deliver letters overnight. The Post Office, however, will do it for a fraction of the cost that FedEx will. Okay, now that I've rationally told you that you're going to save real dollars and cents by using the United States postal Service, you going to dump FedEx? I doubt it. Why? Because you and I both know there's something else going on there.

And that something else is your emotional attachment to a brand that has served you well over the years.

Let's face it, you never hear about FedEx employees going berserk with a shotgun. You never hear about someone discovering sixteen bags of FedEx documents stored in an attic since 1956.

And that's just the dark side of the hidden emotional agenda.

The other side is — and don't tell me this hasn't happened to you — is that people resist abandoning a Big Time Brand, because it's a known quantity with which they've grown familiar and comfortable. I know some people who actually feel guilty about switching away from a brand, as if the company that they've used for the last few years is really going to have its feelings hurt. Fewer defections means lower marketing costs to increase sales from existing end users.

On the positive side, when people invest their emotional loyalty into a brand, it allows you to build the most powerful branding tool there is: *the branded community.* I consider branded community so important, I devoted an entire chapter to it. But for the moment, let's just say that when you own a strong, well-articulated brand, the end-users' loyalty fuses with the evangelism to form an interactive sales force whose mission is first and foremost to promote the success of your brand.

You don't have to search too far to find those brands, either. Apple's Macintosh owns legions of evangelists, as does Starbucks Coffee. These are two strong brands that almost qualify for tax exemption as religions.

Branded communities have all kinds of beauty and wonder, but by far the most wondrous is their ability to defend market share from price-slashing competition. More market share means more sales, more growth, less yelling from the Board of Directors.

Of course, my favorite reason for proposing a strong, well-articulated brand is that when people can articulate how your brand is different, they voluntarily move their purchasing criteria away from a simple price point. The minute they do that, it removes your brand from commodity status.

If that still doesn't make sense to you, look at it this way: if you don't articulate how your brand is different, what other basis are you giving people to use for making their purchasing decision other than price?

I'm old enough to remember that when I was a kid, the coolest sneaker you could buy was called the *P.F. Flyer*. It looked like any other goofy high top. It came in the same dopey colors. But — according to the amphetamine-pumped TV announcer — the *P.F. Flyer* had one thing no other sneaker had: *a built-in flying wedge that made you run faster and jump higher.* Let me tell you pal, I may have been a kid, but the point wasn't lost on me. I was four years old, but at four years of age, about all that matters in life is running faster and jumping higher and I didn't care how many extra hours my dad had to put in at the office, those *P.F. Flyers* were going to be mine.

You think I was going to settle for a cheap set of *Keds*?

Okay, so that's a somewhat oblique example of a brand that has long since decomposed, but you get the point: a well-articulated brand moves you out of the commodity zone. And when you move away from being a commodity, you can command higher rates and better profits.

The Do-It-Yourself Corollary

Alrighty then, I've shown you five very solid ways how a strong, well-articulated brand can make itself known on the bottom line, in real cash. The question now becomes — and I know you're thinking this — how long does it take to see that bottom line getting fat — and how much does it cost?

Let's take the second one first.

The cost of developing a Big Time Brand depends on who's creating the brand for you. And I stress having someone else create the brand because in all my years of branding, I have never seen a successful brand created by the same people who sell the stuff they're branding. Doing it yourself, my friend, works — for suicide. Here's why:

Everyone has a certain skill. Yours is doing what you do. You hire other people to do the stuff you're not so good at, or at the very least, you don't have time to do yourself. Either way, you're doing a huge disservice to your own business when you take yourself away from the business. More importantly, though, branding for *them* means you have to approach your brand from the outside in. Viewing your own company from an outside perspective – free and clear of internal agenda and politics – is fairly impossible. Those who insist on doing their own branding usually end up with an ineffective exercise in corporate puffery, which actually hurts sales more than anything.

The Do-It-Yourself Corollary affects businesses of all sizes, from established multi-nationals to the start-up in the garage next door.

Frankel's Inverse Theory of Branding

Speaking of start-ups, I probably should address the notion of the costs of branding, especially for those of you whose corporate headquarters are conveniently located six feet across the hall from your bedrooms. I'm here to tell you that while branding is truly not a function of finances, it would be totally absurd for me to preach that bucks have nothing to do with it. The clear and simple truth can be best summed up by Frankel's Inverse Theory of Branding, which states:

The smaller your budget, the stronger your brand must be.

The dynamics behind this are fairly straightforward: The way I see it, the stronger, more articulate your brand is, the fewer number of times you have to hammer it through an end-user's head before he gets it. The fewer times you have to hammer it, the lower your marketing costs. And anyone who's ever slept through a business plan knows that the advertising and marketing budgets are what get scrutinized most. People who put money into a business know the differences between costs and revenues, believe me.

In fact, one of the strongest business plans you can write contains a treatise on your what your brand is. After all, if an end user wants to know what he's buying into, don't you think a venture capitalist would be similarly inclined?

Frankel's Inverse Theory of Branding might be ignored by fat cat corporations that reward incompetence on a quarterly basis, but people like you and me can ill afford that kind of luxury. Start-ups and businesses that can't make *Fortune's* 500 cut need marketing strategies and tactics that stick to the wall on the first throw — anything less bankrupts them.

All of which means that the sooner you start your branding, the sooner it pays off — in just about every way you can imagine doing business. Of course, one man's "sooner" is another man's "later", which means that how long it actually takes a brand to impact your bottom line wholly dependent on you. That's right. It all comes down to you again. After all, it's your business. Your schedule. I can tell you right now, though, that the sooner you brand yourself, the quicker it will happen.

With a few conditions.

Which brings us to Frankel's Ubiquitous Brand Test.

Frankel's Ubiquitous Brand Test

I hope that by now, you can see how important this whole branding thing is. I mean, it's everywhere. Or at least it should be. The quickest way to flush all potential increases in revenue is to develop a brand and then ignore it. This has to be among the worst crimes you can commit. I call it Death by Letterhead. A client spends fifty or a hundred thousand bucks developing a great strategy, a superb name and a fabulous execution, only to reduce the entire operation to a new logo slapped on the top of the company stationery.

Is this the way branding is supposed to work? Is this the destiny of a corporate culture? Marooned on a four color logo? Perish the thought.

No, amigo, once you've developed a strong, well-articulated brand, you're going to find that puppy wants to be walked all over your business, poking it's curious head into even the most remote accesses and making its presence felt. And the further you let it wander, the faster it's going to produce.

Here are a couple of examples of branding in action.

Have you ever stayed in a hotel? How about a really nice hotel? One that has soft towels and terrycloth bathrobes? Ever notice the differences between the way operators at a two star hotel and a five star hotel answer the phone? The two star variety usually ask you to hold the line while they connect you. Our five star heroes, on the other hand, connect you and practically ask you out on a date by uttering, "My pleasure." Their pleasure? To gently and delicately connect my phone call! Wow!

I live in Los Angeles, where most relationships are measured by mileage. A quick run-down of which brand ranks where is easily generated by parking policy:

> Street Parking: Lowest quality
> Plenty of Parking Spaces: Low quality
> Plenty of Free Parking Spaces: Average quality
> Valet Parking: Above average quality
> Complimentary Valet Parking: High quality
> Limousine Pick-Up: Top Drawer

To see if you're on the right track, I devised the Ubiquitous Brand Test. A quick reality check to see if you're really letting old Fido do his job. It's short, sweet and goes something like this:

Are we doing it the <brand name> way?

Deceptively simple, eh? Yet this inoffensive litmus test is the best way yet to show you where and how well your brand should be working for you. And don't be shy about pressing it down into the deepest, darkest recesses of your enterprise, either. I've prepared a little checklist for just such an occasion, but feel free to improvise:

How do you answer your telephones?
What do your office forms look like?
What do your marketing materials look like?
What's your corporate culture?
What kinds of partnerships do you pursue?
What kind of gifts do you send your clients/partners?
What kind of promotions do you run?
What type of publicity do you seek?
How does your logo communicate?
How is your terrestrial office decorated?
What does your web site look like?
What kind of community have you built?

Need I go on? The point is that when you brand yourself, you need to brand yourself right on down to the paper clips — are you going to stick with stainless steel or opt for those brightly-colored neon kind?

It makes a statement. It makes a difference. It makes your brand.

The Top Reasons Why Brands Fail

I want to wrap up this chapter by getting a little pro-active on Disaster Avoidance. Too many times, I've watched board members nod their heads knowingly and then go right back to their old, brand-sadistic ways. Don't let this happen to you.

Instead, take a few minutes to memorize the Top Four Reasons Why Brands Fail. Stick them on the wall. Tattoo them someplace private. Do what you have to do, but don't say you weren't warned.

Of course, the overriding reason that brands fail has absolutely nothing to do with money, media or budgets. It has everything to do with you, your company and the people you work with. The fact is that if a strong, well-articulated brand dies, chances are that it rotted from the inside out and no amount of money would have saved it.

But for the record, here they are. The Top Reasons Why Brands Fail:

1 **Strategically Bankrupt:** You've seen it. I've seen it. And a whole chapter on it follows this one. Like I always say, there's no good creative without good strategy and if you create your brand without thinking it through, don't start whining when it falls flat on its face.

2 **Inconsistency:** You've developed a strong brand but haven't deployed it as fully and completely as you need to. The minute you're sold on your brand, let it run rampant over every part of your operation.

Trust me, if it doesn't belong in a particular place, it won't stick for long. But wherever it does stick, it's going to amplify your efforts that much more.

3 Chest-beating: This just goes back to Frankel's First Law of Branding. Enough about you. We know about you. We want to know what you've got for us.

4 Do-it-yourself Disease: Sure, you built the company. And you've gotten it this far. Those are fabulous accomplishments. But your brand — if you've even got one — is dying on the vine. The reason it's hacking and wheezing isn't because you've gone through a steady stream of branding experts, my friend. It's far more likely that you thought branding was pretty much a matter of logo selection.

Well, it's not. And as we fly forward in the brand-intensive economy, trying to develop your brand by yourself has about as high a success rate as removing your own appendix. If you're planning on performing that operation, take the time to become an expert at it. Make sure you do it exactly right.

That 's about as much warning as you're ever going to need. I hope. At least, those are the tactical issues you're going to want to avoid. But being the emotional art that it is, you're going to find that there is an entire army of political issues you're going to run into. It's an ugly, ugly chapter.

In fact, it's the next one.

ACTION ITEMS — CHAPTER FOUR

1. Grab someone in your business and determine your customer acquisition cost.

2. Find someone else to give you your customer repeat and response rates.

3. Shake down your comptroller for a budget to create and implement a brand strategy.

4. Throw a dart at the calendar and pick a date for re-assessing your acquisition, response, repeat and conversion rates.

5. If you decide to launch a brand campaign, read "The Top Reasons Why Brands Fail" to the decision-makers in your group. Get them aboard before you start work.

5

TEN WAYS TO MAKE SURE YOUR BRAND FAILS

There are times when, despite all of your best efforts, your brand just can't seem to get up and fight for your share of market. I can't tell you how many companies have rapped upon my cyber door, complaining about how every million dollars they spend might as well be thrown off a bridge.

"We dumped a half million dollars developing the brand and another five million promoting it — and nothing!" they whimper. It's sad. Disturbing, actually. Because with just a little smarts, a dash of strategic consistency and a fresh dollop of creativity, all of these businesses can be saved.

The problem with most of these brands, incidentally, isn't always the brand itself, but the process by which the poor thing has been developed. Most of the time, in fact, failing brands are doomed long before they ever get out of test market. And over the years, I've developed my own countdown of the top ten ways to absolutely guarantee your brand fails.

10 **The CEO's spouse thinks "it's cute."** Sounds nutty, I know, but the truth of the matter is that a huge number of businesses relegate their marketing issues to the same level of triviality as compiling the annual office Christmas party. If you think I'm kidding, allow me to spin you a yarn from the true annals of advertising, where truth is very often much stranger than fiction. The names, of course, have been changed to prevent innocent authors from getting their butts fried in court.

A long time ago, a major ad agency on the east coast was creating a campaign for a nationally distributed cookie product. The agency had conducted massive market research studies, resulting in reams of reports that, evidently, nobody on the client side had any interest in reading. Being good, strategic creative people, the agency's staff went to work creating storyboards for television commercials, all of which were based on a cogent, consistent strategic direction.

The client, having sat through the entire dog and pony show without flinching, rose from his chair after the presentation and indicated his displeasure by announcing to the stunned conference room, "My wife likes that song Sammy Davis used to sing...what's it called, 'The Sandman' or something?"

It took only a week before the agency attained the rights to "The Candy Man", whereupon the lyrics were changed and the TV spot produced as a popping fresh answer to the Broadway musical. It had nothing to do with cookies. Nothing about consumer issues. And as you may well imagine, did absolutely nothing for sales.

But the CEO's wife really loved it.

9 **The CEO's daughter is majoring in graphic design.** Whoever said that a little knowledge is a dangerous thing must have had branding in mind. Because branding is such a misunderstood issue — even by those "professionals" who practice it — very few people can hold a knowledgeable, cogent discussion about it, much less relate that discussion to the marketing issues at hand. And if the professionals are in that much disarray, you can only imagine how confused the general business public is.

With the dearth of true branding talent comes a huge void that gets filled out of necessity by two types of branding practitioners: those who know very little and those who know even less. And because the two are so indistinguishable, amateurs feel very comfortable stepping into the fray to present their own solutions. The sad truth is that often enough, the work of the amateurs is good enough — or the branding professionals' is bad enough — to render the amateur's work as legitimate marketing. The result is that businesses choose cheap, inexperienced practitioners, figuring they can save a buck or two.

Once again, real branding goes out the window. But the CEO's daughter — who just happens to have submitted the winning entry — coincidentally gets a job with the firm who wins the account.

Don't think I'm kidding. I'm not. What I am doing is showing you just how far from reality most branding and marketing decisions are made, leveraged against issues and agenda that have absolutely no bearing on strategy or planning.

8 **Everyone on the committee agreed on it.** There are some things in life that just can't be done well by committee. Sex is one of them. Branding is another. Yet a large percentage of the companies I find with branding issues seem determined to build their brand from a consensus. Let me tell you right now, nothing contributes to corporate constipation faster than a committee. That's especially true when it comes to developing and creating a brand, and here's why:

Branding is about leadership. It's hoisting your colors above the crowd and motivating them to follow. But leadership is not derived through consensus and compromise. A true leader differentiates himself from the rest of the pack by being different in character, shape and expression. Which is why all the great leaders throughout history have all bordered between heretic and heroic. It's those of us who dare to be different that inspire us to follow. That inspiration translates into motivation and admiration in human beings — why should it apply any differently to a box of power tools?

Of course, while theory may not be politically acceptable in your boardroom, or for that matter, most American places of business, it sure does explain the proliferation of weak, ineffective brands loafing about amidst our culture; these are creatures borne of endless discussions in which *the execution to which the most people don't object to wins.*

The real blood and guts of a brand is borne of the inspirations and motivations that drive an Einstein, a Galileo or Jesus Christ, the former two who disdained committees and the latter of whom was actually done in by one.

If you're going to build a killer brand, don't expect everyone to love it. Don't expect anyone to like it. Because none of them will understand it — at first. That's the way it is with true, worthwhile vision. It's the price you pay for leadership — but it's a price well worth the later rewards.

7 **"It's been that way since we started the company."** In life, everything has its proper place. Conversely, everything that has its place also has a place where it absolutely does not belong. Take, for example, that wonderfully thoughtful portrait your spouse had taken in that somewhat questionable pose. In your wallet, safely tucked away from the prying eyes of your golfing buddies, it's very possibly a good thing. Yet the very same photograph placed squarely on your desk next to your in box could likely get you fired.

It's the same way with the concept of consistency. Consistency has its place. It also has a tendency to get misplaced. Consistency belongs in your strategic planning and execution. But it's definitely out of place when used as an excuse for inaction, or more appropriately, stomping out innovation.

That's when one man's "consistency" becomes a sane man's "stubborn idiocy."

One of the most frequent problems facing stagnant

companies is their misconception of consistency. Most of the time, in fact, the only real consistency lies in the mistakes they keep repeating, simply because "we've always done it that way." The truth is that most business's insistence on status quo has less to do with maintaining consistency than masking the failure of businesses to assume the mantle of leadership.

6The Sales Manager just had 7,500 promotional memos pads printed with the company's logo. You know him. I know him. He's the guy with the plastic pocket protector that racks up six figures worth of frequent flyer miles every twelve months . You gotta love sales guys, because most of the time, they're out on the road or anchored to their desks with telephones wedged into their ears. Nothing happens without sales, it's true.

But sales people aren't marketing people. And confusing the two is a hugely dangerous mistake.

One of the first warning signs that tips me off that a company is in real trouble is when they introduce me to their Vice President of Sales and Marketing. No such thing, Bob. They're two completely different disciplines. Two different species that are impossible to interbreed. That's because salespeople run on the quarter system. They've got to make their numbers every 90 days or die trying. Marketing people, on the other hand, are long term planners. Strategists who understand that building a brand is something that doesn't put cash on the table in 30 days.

Naturally inclined to short term tactics and discretionary promotional budgets, sales guys often are given lots of freedom to travel and do whatever they have to do to bring home the bacon. The problem is that while they're out there bringing home the bacon, they often fail to realize that the home office has gone vegetarian.

Okay, so that one was a little oblique.

What I'm really getting at is that unsophisticated

sales guys tend to work on their own terms, relying on their own skills to churn revenue. The fact is that in their net 30 lives, issues like branding have virtually no effect. So it's not at all unlikely for a sales guy to go out and order a million customized lint brushes without even considering the companies overall branding strategy.

And that's when war breaks out.

Sometime in the staff meeting that he usually misses, the sales guy hears about the company's evolving direction and forcefully objects to the move for "strategic reasons." The truth is that he's already blown 80% of his discretionary promotion budget and is freaking out about how that's going to look on this quarter's financial report.. Waged in front of the CEO, this makes an impressive — if somewhat panicky — presentation of the sales guy's "fiscal responsibility, inevitably having the effect of tabling the branding issue until some time next quarter, when the lint brushes will have been used up.

Meanwhile, the market share continues to slide, because no planning or execution will occur for yet another 90 days. On the other hand, the company can rest easy that its sales prospects will endure the next year in lint-free suits.

5 **The Two Cents Contingent.** If you're ever in a mischievous mood, try this one out around the conference table. It begins with everyone gathering around a conference table for the purported purpose of "getting input" on a particular matter. It doesn't matter what the actual topic is, but for the sake of argument, let's say it's your company's new logo.

Figuring that "we're a company where everyone's opinion counts", you marshal in the troops, all of whom are more than grateful to be involved in an executive decision where brownies and fruit punch are served at no additional cost. In a moment of corporate pride, you unveil the new logo and ask the crowd to go around the room and give you their feedback.

What happens next isn't pretty.

The first thing that happens is that the room falls into two camps: those who think they might get fired and those who are sure of it. You can tell which is which by looking at their eyes, none of which is trained on the logo itself, but zeroing in on every twitching muscle in your face, desperately trying to decode your reactions to their comments.

As the opinions eventually drop out of each reluctant mouth, you'll soon notice that even though you've asked a direct question, you're not getting anything near direct answers. Listen closely and you'll hear non-specific comments about "liking this part" or asking you to explain "why that part has a curly thing in it." You get a large contingent who'll stuff their mouths with brownies and free punch, rendering them unable to voice any opinion at all.

And then there are the "two-cents-ers". People that simply have to throw in their two cents, regardless of how irrelevant their comments may be. These are the folks who believe that by pointing out something negative about anything, they've assured the company of their value. Like Captain Queeg in *The Caine Mutiny*, these guys are convinced that by pointing out some incredibly negative triviality, they'll have saved the company millions in a disaster that might otherwise have occurred.

"Gee, Fred, you sure about that semi-colon? I just read a survey that says literacy rates in America have dropped to the point where...." and so forth. The Two Cents contingent never manages to make a contribution to anything other than the delay and/or destruction of the development process. But it's not their fault. It's yours. Because once again, branding is a leadership issue. It's not a committee decision. It's not a creative decision. It's a strategic decision that belongs solely to visionaries and qualified strategists.

After all of this, if you still feel compelled to have the mailroom staff to feel good about themselves, have them bat first on the company softball team. But don't let them near your branding decisions.

4 Decisions based on "likes" and "dislikes" instead of strategic effectiveness. I'm a stickler for proper terminology. I can't help it, that's the way I am. And with good reason. I remember a day when my kid wanted to go swimming but there were no adults who could be around the pool to watch him. Being my kid, he naturally started to negotiate, asking if he could get his feet wet. I thought about it and figured this was a good way to instill trust in a six year old, and said yes.

Next thing I know, the kid is splashing around in the pool, diving like a dolphin and having the time of his life. I started yelling at him, "Hey, I thought we agreed you could get your feet wet!"

"But Dad," he replied, "They *are* wet."

What's the point to this story? One, I have a clever kid. Two, the standards by which you judge a brand demand just as much precision as a kid in a swimming pool. Too many times, a brand is judged by what people like instead of if it works.

People like all sorts of things. They like roses, Barry Manilow and long walks on the beach. They even like head cheese and pork rinds. But branding isn't about what people like — at least not initially. Branding is about what works. Of course, people will like a brand, but only when it works. They like it because it strategically fits with their wants and communicates that fit in a compelling way. You can like your own brand, too, but only when it works by bringing your target market wagging their hard-earned cash.

All too often, I hear people offering up their opinions as to what they like and don't like. That's fine. But when it comes to branding, the sure way to fail is by basing your decisions on what you like best, rather than what works best.

3 **Brand has not evolved with the company (Pushcart Syndrome)** If you're this far into the book, you've come to acknowledge that a brand is far more than a corporate symbol that squats in the middle of your business card. A brand is your corporate personality, its culture and its temperament. Few people realize that the term "incorporation" was developed to embody all the faculties found in a regular human being without actually *being* a human being.

But businesses are very human and as such, they grow. They change. And the brand they wear must change with them. It's a careful balancing act, but failing to keep a brand current — or changing it too radically — can destroy any brand in a heartbeat.

The most common occurrence is what I call the Pushcart Syndrome, where Poppa founded the business a few generations ago, selling his widgets door-to-door out of a pushcart. Back then, a marketing campaign boiled down to who could yell the loudest across the street. Thanks to hard work and perseverance, the old man grew the business and put his four sons through college. These days, the boys run four regional divisions that span the country. The only trouble is that they still think and act like Poppa with his pushcart — and everywhere they display it, their brand reinforces it.

Sure, tradition and establishment have their place. But improperly branded, an outdated communication becomes one that falls on deaf ears and results in eroding market share. Still not convinced? Here's a real life example:

A church near my neighborhood couldn't figure out why their membership kept eroding. It seems that the older generation who first established the church was beginning to die out, and their sons and daughters weren't particularly drawn by the same issues as their parents once were. The church administrators were worried, and rightly so, because they understood that they could no longer rely on a dying population to support their institution.

The problem, of course, was their brand image. The church had grown from a small center for religious services into a large community, but the administrators failed to incorporate that fact into their thinking. The church elders, having founded the institution, remained steadfast in their belief that their appeal to churchgoers at large lay in the personal attributes of one or two of their highest priests. They had become so mired in their traditional comfort zone that they completely missed the way in which the church's community and social aspects had totally eclipsed its religious attributes. The little old building with an intimate, loyal and obedient flock had long since grown into several buildings, overflowing with modern day families and children, laughing and learning in a day school. The institution's reputation as a vast repository of intellectual wealth had become world renown.

And yet membership was declining.

The reason the membership was declining was that the administrators refused to acknowledge that *their* perception of the church and the reality of *what the public wanted* were no longer in synch. The public wanted to identify with an institution associated with world class philosophers and intellectual learning. What they were being stuck with was the priest's refusal to grow with them — Poppa's pushcart — so the public has begun to look elsewhere.

A brand that doesn't keep pace with its business is even worse than having no brand at all, because instead of communicating nothing, it communicates the wrong thing. And that's one of the most lethal branding mistakes anyone can commit.

2 **Brand has millions, but no value.** One of the most powerful enemies a brand can have is a huge advertising budget. I know, it sounds like a problem we'd all love to have, but in terms of branding, Frankel's Second Law of Marketing clearly states that the more money you have, the lazier you get. And nowhere is this truer than with a business's brand issues.

Of course, this is wonderful news for all of you beleaguered souls who find that your children's lunch budgets dwarf your own marketing budget, because it lets you know that all the money in the world won't do anything for you if your brand isn't effective at communicating your company's attributes. Essentially, the converse of Frankel's Second Law is also true: the less money you have, the smarter you have to be. And that's where the best brands can often be found.

In America, we're all conditioned to think like Tevye from *Fiddler On The Roof*, who opines, "it doesn't make one bit of difference if I answer right or wrong. When you're rich they think you really know." Not that I derive all my wisdom from Broadway musicals, but the observation couldn't be truer than in the world of branding. And if you doubt that, just take a look at some of the more popular "brands" out there today.

Sure, you know names like Nike, McDonald's and even Coca-Cola. You use brands like Microsoft and Levi's. But think for a minute as to *why* you use those brands and chances are you'll find that you use them out of familiarity rather than anything else. The reason why those brands are so familiar is that all of these companies spend gazillions of dollars promoting their brands, without really communicating anything about them.

When you really get down to it, you'll find that all of these "brands" aren't really brands at all, but well-moneyed names that bank on familiarity rather than key consumer issues. That's why you and I know damn well that you certainly would stop at the Burger King rather than McDonald's, you'd chug the Pepsi if there were no Coke and grab a pair of marked-down Adidas instead of the Nikes the first chance you got.

Lots of money and spending it: one hallmark of a weak brand.

1 **Brand doesn't compel target prospects.** A distant cousin of the well-moneyed-but-ineffectual brand, the most tragic case of brand failure is, well, not unlike Bill Gates himself: powerful, but not terribly compelling. There was a time when all a brand had to be was somewhat strategic and a tad communicative. Those were the same days, incidentally, that it took a month to hear the news that President McKinley was just shot.

These days, news is received pretty much as it happens. There's less and less time lag between cause and effect, which mean the really killer brands can't afford to sit around smoking cigars waiting for the market to warm to their glow.

Oh, I can hear all the old farts groaning that a brand is a brand, and that brand *positioning* is really what I'm talking about. Well, that's not what I'm talking about at all. What I'm talking about is the very core of my branding being. It's the fact that simply stating who you are, or why our market should choose you over your competition is no longer sufficient for establishing a compelling brand. That theory worked fine when Lindy made it to Paris, but these days, the market wants to know what's in it for them — and they want to know right now.

For that reason, a brand has to contain a compelling proposition right there in the middle of its forehead, in a way that the market finds completely comprehensible and motivating. If the market doesn't see your brand as the only solution to their problem, you haven't got a compelling brand. Merely inviting your market to choose your brand over your competition is actually an invitation to the competition to join in a review — essentially asking your competitors to take a shot at stealing your prospect — and why would you ever want to do that?

Nevertheless, the vast majority of marketing and branding "experts" allow their clients to do just that, by not insisting that the brand be compelling enough to be perceived properly by the target prospects, which is another surefire way to cripple your brand.

And that's why branding and marketing people have the reputations they do.

ACTION ITEMS — CHAPTER FIVE

1. Go through all ten items to familiarize yourself with the territory and see how they apply to your company's internal political structure.

2. Make a list of five more ways that your company in particular might derail your efforts.

3. Write down counter-strategies for each.

4. Write down a strategic battle plan for creating a "buy-in" for the brand strategy — after you create it, how will you motivate the rest of the troops to get behind it?

5. Create a reward system for early adopters based on embracing and implementing the brand strategy.

6

WHAT'S IN A NAME?

A lot of people — my father, included — still don't really understand what I do for a living. You have no idea how tough it is for my poor wife when we're at parties and the conversation turns to what-my-husband-does-for-a-living kind of stuff. It's so easy for all the other women to rattle off their husbands' occupations. I mean, how tough is it to explain to your dinner mate what a proctologist is?

Or for that matter, *does*?

It's different with branding guys. Because branding is the most misunderstood concept in and around the marketing world, it's even harder to explain what it is or how to do it. But I'll try.

Let me start out by stating I believe that everyone in life has a God-given gift. In almost every case, every human being has a gift they can exploit to a greater degree than the dopes sitting next to them. Some people can explain the direct correlation between matter and energy. Others can fart an entire fugue on key. At the very least, every person has the capacity to be themselves better than anyone else on the planet.

My gift to the world is making people see things from a different perspective. One way that gift manifests itself by naming things.

Most people confuse brands with names. To be sure, you can't have a brand without one, but a name is only part of the totality of a brand. Nevertheless, it probably bears taking a few moments to talk about them. How to create them and how to tell if they're any good once you've created them.

Right off the bat, the biggest mistake that most people make when it comes to naming things is slapping a terse definition on them. Names like *Nutri-grain* might tell you what a product is, but does it really tell you anything about why you should invest your loyalty there?

I also have no idea why businesses take so much pride in misspelling words, jamming them together and them passing them off as brands. Does *Rite-Aid* make your mouth water? What about *NyQuil*? *Weed-B-Gone*? Do these names do anything at all to cultivate an allegiance from you?

The next most common mistake is inventing some weird term that sounds scientific but means nothing at all. Usually, it's the cloning of two or more product benefits that have been genetically altered and fused back together in some god-forsaken board meeting. The result is a name that sounds as if it were created on the *Island of Dr. Moreau*; half-cat, half-dog. Complete violations of nature.

Names like *Omnicom* , which must have something to do with communicating to everything or everyone. Which is odd, because it actually communicates nothing to anyone. Or that travel agency from outer space, *Uniglobe*. When you stop and think about it, it really means "one globe."

Right. As if that's going to get you to pick up the phone and plan a trip.

The part that these guys have forgotten is that names — like the brands they represent — are *emotional* creatures. They have to inspire, entertain and communicate. But more than that, they have to win the prospects' hearts. And you don't do that with dopey puns and misspellings that sends end-users' eyes spinning back into their heads. You do it with charm. A little wit. A little twinkle in the eye.

And a whole lot of strategy.

In case you were wondering, I should tell you that there are a bunch of brand names that I think are totally Big

Time. One of the most popular soft drinks in the late 1980's was *Jolt* cola, a very cool little brand with a lightning bolt stabbed through the heart of its label, reminding its consuming public that it contained "the highest levels of caffeine allowed by law." Wow. Talk about imagery. Talk about being hard-wired into the brains of your psychographics.

As long as we're on the topic of sodas, *New York Seltzer* was another brand name whose imagery sold it over better-moneyed competition. The fact that neither of these brands is as popular today has nothing to do with their branding. Even well-branded companies make silly business decisions. The watchword is *growth* and both of these brands began as independents that flourished where few before had even dared to tread. Moreover, both of these brands enjoyed huge, nay rabid, brand loyalty in their heyday.

Which brings me to my next point.

Nothing wrong with a little fun.

.

Is there anything written in any book that says that your brand can't be fun? That it can't bring a little joy and humor into the lives of those it touches? Of course not. Yet to look at the brands that most of corporate America cranks out, you'd think that boredom and mediocrity are what powers mindshare. One of the least-heralded contributions of the web culture, by the way, is that it has brought back a little bit of mischief to mass market branding. It's gotten gray-haired men in five hundred dollar loafers to talk about companies like *Yahoo* while trying keep to a straight face.

Throughout the ages, the brands that capture the hearts and minds of the end using public are those that bring a little touch of humanity along with their selling proposition. Snack food, in particular, went through this craze in the late sixties with really cool brands like *Onyums, Doodles* and so forth. One brand in particular was so damn memorable and fun it actually made a comeback in the nineties . It happens to be one of my favorite names of all time, incidentally: *Screaming Yellow Zonkers.*

Look, the average Joe works forty or fifty hours a week just to feed his wife and kids. He's got more worries about drugs and crime and how he's going to make the next mortgage payment. In a world where depression runs rampant, you can bet that shining your little love light on folks doesn't hurt your brand image one bit. Neither does cracking a few jokes or a gentle tug of the heartstrings.

If you doubt the veracity of my claims, try testing it out yourself. Ask any adult over the age of 35, for example, about *Tang.* I'm going to bet that even though the television commercials haven't aired in over twenty years, every person who remembers the brand will tell you — with a warm, reminiscent smile — that *Tang is the orange juice that the astronauts drank.*

What a great concept. A product that was probably more sugar and orange food coloring than anything else, sold itself on pure imagery and a fun name. I'm sure that someone tried to kill it for that very reason, mind you, which is why the product was positioned as a *tangerine* juice product. The name, purportedly, was just a contraction.

To this day, however, I'm convinced that fun was what sold it.

I also prefer brands that don't take themselves seriously. It seems to me that ever since the Warren report, too many people spend too much of their time trying to ferret out bad news. It's gotten to be a national pastime. With lawyers suing everyone to whom they can throw a summons, America seems to have gotten into this weird, paranoid frame of mind. For decades, everyone has been so afraid to commit themselves to anything other than the straight and narrow, that we've forgotten how to relax and enjoy.

For that reason, de-stressing brands are among my

favorites. These are brands that are forthright enough to admit, "Hey, you know this is no big deal and we know this is no big deal, so let's just get through this and go have a beer." One of my favorite de-stressed brands comes — surprisingly enough — from one of the most uptight straight-and-narrow brands in America: Hallmark greeting cards.

Shoebox Greeting Cards bills itself as "a tiny division of Hallmark," which to me, borders on genius. I say genius, because *Shoebox* is obviously the black sheep of Hallmark, printing the stuff that coastal types eat up with a fork and Midwesterners spit out in disgust. In a brilliant move, Hallmark realized that it could crank out *Shoebox* cards as its own brand, keeping arm's length from its edgy content while maintaining its own apple pie image. A well-crafted brand, *Shoebox* creates and maintains its rebel image while credibly linking with its end users' emotions. *Shoebox* cards say the stuff we wish we could say, but lack the courage.

It's a Big Time Brand.

Perhaps the hardest habit to break with names is the notion that the name has to communicate what your brand actually does. While your name certainly should transmit — or at least hint at — what you're foisting on an unsuspecting public, there's more to it than that. Attitude plays a big role in transmitting the personality of a brand, especially on the web, where culture has sprung from informality. A perfect example of this is the occasion upon which a good friend of mine wanted to build a site for her boyfriend, Bob, as a gift, which I thought was a whole lot more useful than the traditional J.C. Penney necktie. In any case, Bob was a professional music guy who scored video games and movies. My friend wanted to build a site that showcased his music.

I suppose she could have called the site *bobmusic.com.* Or *bobtunes.com.* But neither of those really captured the essence of the guy. He struck me as a talented musician whose personality could run from the sensitive to the whimsical. Which is why I thought *dumdeddumdum.com* was a whole lot more appropriate. True, it didn't contain anything whatsoever to with Bob's name, but I had a great time imagining people saying the name to themselves, chuckling about it, and then telling their friends.

Which is what branding is all about.

Another online brand that I think fills the bill is *theknot.com*. Unless you've been there, you really wouldn't know what it is or what it's about. But once you've declared your betrothal to another, you understand that it's the site for all things wedding. Sure, they could have called it *every-bride.com* or *weddingtown.com*. But they didn't. They hung their personality on a colloquial hook that said everything it had to say without ever saying it.

Getting Personal

Before we get too far down the road, I want to address the one instance that's almost always a sure fit, both branding and name-wise: personal services. Using your own name to brand yourself is perfectly acceptable.

Well, not perfect, but pretty darn close.

The best reason for using your own name as your brand is that, for the most part, you're the only one who can fulfill its promise. I say for the most part, because to their chagrin, there are other Rob Frankels in the world who probably wish they owned *robfrankel.com*, the brand with which I associate myself. Too bad. I got there first. I didn't, however, beat the rush to 1-800-ROBFRANKEL, but did manage to get 1-888-ROBFRANKEL. I have no idea who owns the 800 version, but if they're reading this right now, I'll spiff you 10% for any branding work you refer to me.

My point is that part of being the "only solution" is easily fulfilled by being yourself. And if you're running a business in which the major product offering is your personal service, I believe using your name as your URL is the best way to go. It looks more professional, sounds more substantial and at the very least, isn't cute and punny as so many sole proprietors tend to be. There must be at least three million copywriters online who undermine their brand quality by promoting themselves with cheap wordplays like *the copy shop, wordsrus* or something equally insulting.

Be better than that. People who react to great names react even more strongly to bad ones. That's why Marion Morse changed his name to John Wayne and Reginald Dwight became Elton John. If you've secured your own name, by all means use it in your URL, your e-mail address, your toll-free telephone number and just about anything else you can stick it on.

There's only one you. And nothing drives that point home more clearly than knowing that no matter where in the world they may be, whoever types your name into his browser will bring him directly to your front door.

ACTION ITEMS — CHAPTER SIX

1. Make a list of four other names besides your own and put them on a list.

2. Include at least one that is so off-the-wall/fun that you're positive nobody in their right mind would possibly take it seriously.

3. Ask someone — preferably someone who doesn't know you — to describe what each name means to them.

4. Ask that same person — in a different question — which one they *like* best, the term "like" meaning which one sounds the most accessible and friendly to them.

5. Look at yourself in the mirror. Come up with five new names for yourself that you think would convey the traits about you most people enjoy. If you really want to have fun, think of a real creep at the office and come up with five compelling and descriptive names for him.

7

BEFORE & AFTER

I suppose that by Chapter 7, you'd be getting a tad restless about a guy spouting off about branding without showing you the goods. I know I certainly would. Heck, it's easy to shred everyone else's work. The tough part is coming through and proving yourself just as everyone else is convinced you're full of beans.

Well, we're short on beans today.

Chapter 7 is about real, live branding problems and solutions. I want to take you through a few of them. But before I do, here are the ground rules:

First, I want you to keep in mind that in each case — just as in your own — the brands are not designed for universal appeal. By that, I mean they're designed to play within the confines of each client's universe. And that's a terribly important realization for you to factor into your own branding. In fact, it takes the form of Frankel's First Law of Common Sense, which states:

Brand to an audience who realistically might buy.

If you're in the bug spray business, there's little point in vying for world brand domination outside that sphere of influence. The people you want to target are those whose lives are touched by bug spray in a meaningful, fairly regular way. Little girls in party dresses don't care about bug spray, nor do professional bungee-jumpers. Exterminators care. Homemakers care. Perhaps gardeners. But aloft in Air Force One, it is doubtful that the President of the United States is staying up late tonight worrying about roaches in the kitchen.

The point is to frame your branding expectations within a realistic parameter. All of the following examples certainly do.

The second point I want you to remember is that no two clients are ever alike. All of them have their own problems. They all have varying goals and find themselves struggling with ever-changing market conditions. So I'm going to set up each of the case studies with all of that information. That way, you can better apply your situation to theirs.

Lastly, I've deliberately selected brands ranging from national and international status down to the very smallest, local start-up, in an effort to show you how budget and everything else those MBA's blame your misfortunes upon really doesn't matter at all.

Ready?

1 **The International Real Estate Franchise.** For those who have been living in caves for the past few decades, RE/MAX is an internationally-franchised real estate organization that revolutionized the industry with their 100% commission strategy. Up until their debut, almost every real estate agent in the world lay at the mercy of their realty broker, who charged them upwards of 70% of every commission on every piece of real estate they bought or sold. RE/MAX's stroke of genius was to completely eliminate that structure and allow the agents to keep every penny of their commissions. All the agent had to do was pay the RE/MAX broker for the office space and support offered by RE/MAX.

Pretty revolutionary, eh?

Going from a 30% share to 100% commission structure was all that the really motivated agents needed to hear and within a few years, all the movers and shakers were leaving the standard brokerages and racing over to join

RE/MAX. The result was that within a short time, RE/MAX had attracted enough of these "top producers" to independently verify that "the average RE/MAX agent out-produces the average real estate agent by a margin of three to one."

That's pretty good. So what was their brand positioning?

"RE/MAX. Above the crowd." With a balloon.

Above the crowd!

Huh?

I don't always create brand names for clients and in this case, there was no way that they were going to change it. But in its own oblique way, if you stared at it long enough, I figured that the name communicated enough to the people at whom in was aimed: the "RE" stood for "real estate" and the "MAX" stood for...maximum, I suppose. Both were targeted concepts. But there was a major disconnect in the way the brand name was positioned.

Adding to the mix was the requirement that the brand had to appeal equally to real estate agents and the end users who employed them. People who bought and sold their homes needed to know what RE/MAX stood for and why.

"Above the crowd." Yeesh. If there ever was an oblique, chest-beating phrase, this had to be it. It had nothing to do with real estate. No association with RE/MAX. No compelling interest for either consumers or agents.

It took a strong leadership effort on the part of the California franchise, but eventually I devised the positioning that carried the message through to both targets with equal strength:

RE/MAX: THE MAXIMUM REAL ESTATE HAS TO OFFER.

Okay, *now* we're talking. You want end user benefits? You got 'em — on three different levels. Real estate agents get their maximum commissions. Franchise owners open more offices that draw even more high-performing producers. Consumers get the maximum performance out of their agents because we showed them our guys outperformed the average real estate agent by a margin of 3 to 1.

It worked, big time. In television, print, radio and especially in developing the esprit de corps that made up the RE/MAX community. It worked so well, in fact, that the California franchise actually recouped a portion of its investment by reselling its newly branded materials to other franchises across the country.

2 Catering to Hollywood Hidden away within the nepotistic fiefdom that is Hollywood, are thousands of enterprises yearning to be touched by the magic of dream merchants. Among those vying for their affections in the land of Let's-Do-Lunch are the people who feed the movie magnates. After all, even the Beautiful People have to eat.

Or at the very least, binge and purge.

No matter. If you're caterer in Hollywood, the name

of the game is to serve as many important names as you do main courses. The idea is that being the lemming-driven community it is, it only takes one dinner at the Studio or luncheon at a celebrity's home to make or break your reputation.

In Hollywood, once you're in, you're in. And once you're out, you never were.

The race to feed Hollywood faces is tough and extremely competitive. It is not uncommon, for example, to lose money on a celebrity event in order to rack up more business (on which caterers often lose even more). But if you do manage to snag an important event, it's like hitting the lottery: you get to charge ridiculous amounts of money for incredibly small portions. People actually clamor for your calendar and put up with the very worst service you can possibly offer.

I know. It's weird. But it's Hollywood.

Now that I've defined the culture into which Encore Catering found itself, you may be able to better appreciate the situation in which they found themselves. There, in the midst of the most cliquish, simple-minded and intolerant community on the planet, Encore was swimming upstream with this as their brand:

Hmmm. Hardly the stuff of dreams, is it?

Encore Catering was another micro-business whose marketing budget was slightly smaller than their phone bill, which meant that branding was especially important to them. Again, the client had no intention of abandoning the name "Encore."

Encore's chief strategy was to cater to the show business community, but nothing about their brand conveyed that concept. So the first step was to identify exactly how Encore wished to be perceived by its prospects — and then present themselves as the solution for that community. The way I advise a client to do that is by writing down a simple sentence in the most boring, dry fashion imaginable. No cleverness. No puns. No advertising. Just say what you mean. And here's what we wrote:

If you're in the movie industry,
we're the catering specialists for you.

I know it sounds amazingly simple, but at the time, while there were dozens of caterers who specialized in food, there simply were no other caterers who specialized in the *industry*. The real solution came in the realization that this target audience was far more concerned with their affairs from a business point of view rather than a culinary one.

It was about making the *event* a success — not food. I find that happens a lot: it's not so much *what* you're selling, but *how you sell it* that counts. That's where the brand really lives.

This was one of the assignments that required a new corporate identity, as well, to wit:

Ah, that's better.

Well, you certainly couldn't miss that we were talking about food here. But notice that we never showed food. We showed an *empty* plate whose contents had obviously been wolfed down by a very satisfied — or hungry — patron. That communicated success, which was what our audience was after.

The tagline positioning the brand became "We keep them coming back for more." A double duty line that the sales team was able to merchandise two ways. On the one hand, party goers kept coming back to the buffet tables for more food. On the other, Encore clients kept coming back to them to cater additional events, which substantiated their claims of referral business.

Finally, the corporate identification classed up the company personality and tone. By appearing more professional, the company was accepted as more professional by a very small, tightly-knit community.

A tasty example, if I say so myself.

3 **Wireless From the Ground Up.** There are some choice occasions on which a client has a fabulous product or service and nothing else. Those are the plums that are ripest for branding, because there's no legacy to inherit. No biases. No traditions. No pre-conceived notions.

Just pure, raw, unadulterated commodity.

Those are the branding challenges I prefer, personally, And that's what I was lucky enough to begin with when Vanguard Communications approached me with their newest service. Vanguard had started its operations by introducing wireless cable television to Southern California. The service had a lot going for it, but it had a few challenges to go along with it. To begin with, the company had expanded its range of services from cheaper, higher quality wireless cable television to providing cheaper, higher quality telephony services, as well. It also took the revolutionary approach of cutting building owners in on the profits generated from each tenant.

What Vanguard needed was a new name. A Big Time Brand.

Here's what they got:

The name OpTel was a contraction for "Optimal Telecommunications", under which we claimed "the choice is clear." And it was. For end-users, their telephone and television signals were remarkably clearer than land lines. The programming and services were less expensive, too. The building owners had no problem with that and were especially motivated to choose OpTel because it was the only company to share its revenues with them (incidentally, the dots represented the straight-line microwave transmissions that OpTel aimed at building antennae to receive its signals. In cases where a direct line of sight wasn't available, OpTel actually bounced the signal like a cue ball off the nearest structures, banking the signal until it fell into the dish).

For everyone concerned, the choice really was clear. Especially the focus groups who tested the name, ranking it behind Pacific Bell as "the second most established brand they remembered" — a full three months before the brand was even launched.

4 **A Concrete Example.** While it is true that a fair amount of my branding clients are technologically-driven products and services, the bulk of my practice is composed of mostly analog businesses. And when you're talking non-digital, it's hard to beat the cement-coating industry.

Sundek Systems is a beautiful example of a brand that had stalled in the marketplace. Their business consisted of decorative coatings poured over existing concrete decks and patios. By using their product, you not only beautified your yard, patio or hotel entrance, but also saved boatloads of money by not having to remove, re-pour and replace your old concrete .

In the early 1970's this was a revolutionary idea and the company grew steadily into a national enterprise. Through the 1980's Sundek enjoyed a position as a market leader. But in the 1990's the company began to notice an erosion in that position.

Their brand had obviously been neglected since its early days:

One look told you all you needed to know about why their market share was in danger. In the first place, there was no communication, no hint as to what the company produced. In the second, the company ignored the importance of its graphical identity, committing the error of utilizing fonts and symbols that were hopelessly out-of-date. Now, I'm not one to be cutting edge about anything, mainly because the minute you become cutting edge, someone else has figured out a way to re-cut it. But in Sundek's case, it seriously damaged their credibility in their claim to be a market leader. Imagery and design rooted in the 1960's contradicted any message about being current in the present.

But there was a more serious issue at stake here.

Sundek had taken its position as the market inventor — they created the category — and relied on its market to make the quantum leap. They relied on the market to equate inventiveness with premium quality. What they failed to realize is that by not articulating why Sundek was a better solution, they were vulnerable to smaller, lower-priced competitors.

Indeed, Sundek's market perception was that of "the guys who invented concrete coatings." But it didn't progress much past the point of 40 pound bags of cement. The truth of the matter is that Sundek had a variety of attributes that it had never sold. Product and service characteristics that had real meaning to both Sundek resellers and end-users.

The main task was shifting Sundek's brand away from a perceived commodity to a company backed by a total commitment to its customers. By emphasizing the services customers received at no extra cost, Sundek's premium prices became more of a value. By showcasing the dedication to improving their products on a constant schedule, resellers now had a point of difference that moved prospects away from price.

That's what I used to reposition their brand.

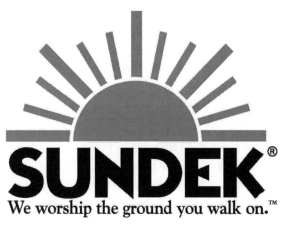

One example in particular that I found effective was the suggestion of doing away with the "lifetime guarantee." The phrase had been so overused as to be regarded as completely meaningless by most consumers. I did, however, recommend that Sundek offer to guarantee their products and services "for one hundred years." That certainly sparked more interest.

Gradually, Sundek came to realize that although it offered its products to the world, in its competitive environment, it would have to offer them more than that. The people at Sundek saw that by adding services — and featuring them — they could provide end users with more reasons to choose Sundek as their solutions — most of which went unmatched by their competitors.

This new brand positioned Sundek as a premium player in their market, in which premium prices would eventually parlay into higher margins — and happier resellers.

5 **The Gift That Keeps on Giving.** A substantial number of the clients I help are start-ups, which I actually prefer. There's nothing quite like taking an idea from concept to reality. And when you're launching a new business, part of that process involves naming it. Names are a critical element of a brand and if I'm lucky, I can get to a business before they've finally settled in on theirs. This is one case where I managed to slide in just under the bell.

The good news was that I had gotten a call regarding a new business that was about to launch online. The bad news was that it was a gift shop. At the time, shopping online was just catching on and everyone with ten free megabytes of hard disk space was fashioning themselves as the online answer to K-Mart.

That wasn't the worst of it, though.

The worst part was that this was a gift site. And in the very first wave of shopping sites that went online, the first ones to wash up on the shoreline were gift sites. There were way too many of them and none of them were very compelling. In order to survey the situation, I was given the following URL to click:

dreamcatalog.com

Like you, I figured that this was a catalog of astral projection experiences. Or some sort of sleep fantasy. But it turned out that the designers had really intended the site to be "the catalog of dream gifts," which still didn't explain why it featured sofa lounges floating over moonscapes and lava lamps set in Amazon jungles.

There was clearly a lot of work to be done.

The first order of business was to figure out how a gift site with no price advantage and no clear niche could possibly distinguish itself from the rest of the herd. The second item on the agenda was to give the site a compelling name that communicated its benefit to its end users. Once again, by positioning the brand as the only solution to the end users' problems, we were able to hammer out the following strategy:

A gift isn't about what you buy.
It's about the expression on the face of its recipient.

Now that was a solution. A brand whose entire purpose hinged on its buyers' ability to run around and purchase gifts based solely on the reactions they elicited from recipients. Suddenly, a whole culture sprang up from a new site with a new name:

ILoveThatGift!com

Tagged with a promise of "100% Guaranteed Joy", the entire site resonated with the promise of gift-giving success. People who purchased gifts from our inventory were far more assured that the people to whom they sent gifts would enjoy them, because that's the way we bought them. Instead of selling items, the site was selling its ability to give you the right solution to your gift-giving problem.

We were guaranteeing the *joy of the recipient* instead of the merchandise.

So there you have a few samples ranging from the eensy-weensy to international. All of them were radically off kilter when I found them. Some of them had already kissed away millions in advertising budgets. Others hadn't quite made it out of the gate yet. But every single one of them will continue on a clearer, more efficient path if they stick to the brands we constructed.

Every brand I've showcased here — regardless of size — can merchandise its brand qualities and strengths into it culture. Each can invent and build new services and profit centers. Each can nurture and grow its own branded community, based on a clear, well-articulated brand.

The very same way you can.

It's not about budget. It's about branding.

ACTION ITEMS — CHAPTER SEVEN

1. List all the attributes that you think your company has to offer.

2. Have someone else — someone you trust from outside your company — make another list, on another piece of paper, of why they value your company.

3. Compare the two lists and see how they match — or more likely — *don't* match up.

4. Try coming up with extra products and services that are based on the outsider's list.

5. Pretend your business is a religion. Who are the high priests, what do they look like and how would they conduct a service to bring a new product into the world?

6. More importantly, how would they keep the flock from marrying outside the faith?

7. If you don't like the religion analogy, try the same tactic using an alien civilization from Mars.

8

OKAY, LET'S TALK ABOUT YOU
The Mantle of Leadership

Iwant to take a minute and mention an important aspect of branding that has absolutely nothing to do with marketing or strategy or the latest numbers from your brown-nosing research director. It's the most human part of branding and despite its rank on my list of laws, it's so vital, so critical to your branding success that it merits its own law.

What makes this law so critical is that it's the only law I've got that rests squarely on your shoulders. It has nothing to do with your customers. Or the media. Or even your board of directors.

This is the one time where it really is all about you.

To really appreciate this, you have to go back to your school days. I mean your really early school days. Back when really beautiful young school teachers gave you a gold star for raising your hand instead of blurting out a question. Remember that? How about following in a single file line? Not talking in class?

Now fast forward a bit to young adulthood. Remember law and order? That early morning trip home from the poker game where you were the only car on the road and you stopped at the red light for three minutes?

Well, you're an adult now. And if you're like the rest of us, they did their best to stomp out whatever individuality you were born with. We all grow up that way. We're taught to follow the rules. To fit in. To *not* attract attention. That's why, incidentally, more people fear public speaking than they do death. We've all been trained to blend into the wallpaper and not make any trouble.

And that is the least talked-about aspect of successful branding.

In order to really crank your brand, you must be comfortable with being different than the rest. In fact, you have to be proud enough to brag about it. You have to reach back into your childhood and convince yourself that being the first kid to wear braces didn't make you a geek but a trendsetter. A visionary.

You have to accept the fact that the world doesn't readily accept leaders and is, for the most part, jealous of them. Which brings me to Frankel's Sixth Law of Branding:

The success of a brand varies directly with the ability to accept the mantle of leadership.

Branding — really strong branding — tweaks the noses of society and dares to go its own way. It may sound fun and romantic, but in reality, it can get pretty lonely. You can feel as if you're leading a parade with nobody following. You can know in your heart that your cause is right, but nobody's listening. It gets pretty discouraging.

Until.

Until that day when someone, somewhere makes the connection. You make your first hit. Then three more. Then ten and twenty. And pretty soon, you're airborne. A leader.

That's the way it is with leadership. It's not for the fainthearted, but it is incredibly rewarding. Creating a strong, sustainable brand is directly proportional to your belief in that brand and yourself and all that you create. So before you set out to create that branded presence, do a reality check. Make sure that kid with the braces knows he's a hero.

That last part is really inspirational, isn't it? You know why it's so empowering? Because it allows you to feel great about the parts of you that aren't like everyone else. After years of repression, it lets you enjoy your differences instead of feeling ashamed of them. For the first time, you can feel good about the fact that you *don't* fit in.

Welcome to branding.

If you can wrap your brain stem around the fact that being different is good, you're halfway home to building a Big Time Brand. The other half is just a chip shot away, in the form of Frankel's Fourth Law of Branding, which simply states:

Build from your strengths.

I can't tell you how many strategy meetings I sit through where everyone sits around the table whining about what their competitors are offering. Don't get me wrong. I'm all for competitive research and analysis. You've got to know who the players are and what kind of shenanigans they're up to. What I'm *not* in favor of is competitive obsession. The constant hand-wringing and worry over what they're doing and when they're doing it.

The reality is that you wouldn't be in business if you didn't have a plan or resource that you felt was strong enough to make a difference. Something real enough on which to build a business. And if your difference is at all innovative, it has to be something that nobody else is doing — which by definition means that nobody else can claim it.

Now if you go to all that trouble to create and market that difference, why on earth wouldn't you want to lead with that difference? Yet time after time, that's exactly the type of corporate shrinkage I see. Instead working from their strengths, too many businesses undermine their brands by trying to play catch-up with their competitors.

In my book, if you manufacture Red better than anyone else when everyone else is chunking out Blue, you shouldn't be wasting your time and resources figuring out a way to crank out Blue. You do Red. Do it better than anyone else and you'll do better, for a few reasons:

1 Your brand is based on the fact that you've come up with a way to make Red a better solution for your end user. So you have reality on your side to begin with. That's your strength.

2 If you do Red better and your competition does Blue, don't be a schmuck: let them have Blue. They do it better. They're more established. They've devoted more resources to it. For you to get into Blue is going to cost you plenty and dilute your efforts. If you go for Blue, Red will suffer.

3 If you dilute your efforts, you're going to confuse your end-users.

4 If you've hooked into the notion that the media is becoming more psychographically-driven, you know that people who want Red search for Red, not Blue.

What it really boils down to is that when you combine the qualities of leadership and strength that Big Time Branding requires, the picture you get resembles something out of a John Wayne movie. You've got to keep your head down and your aim real straight.

And for God's sake, stop listening to everyone.

It's your vision. Your innovation. Don't expect anyone to understand it until the market proves you right. Then have your secretary handle all the congratulatory calls from the folks "who were behind you all the way from the beginning."

Yeah, right.

Work from your strengths. Flaunt them. Tattoo them all over the market and especially your operation. Make them permanent. Solid.

Which reminds me: can we talk about logos?

A logo is a logo. A brand is a brand.

If you bounce around the web as much as I do — and even if you don't — you're going to run into one of the most basic branding issues out there. It's that old favorite of how and when to use a logo.

To begin with, let's clear the decks with the notion that a logo and a brand are not the same thing. A brand defines who you are, what you do, how you do it and why anyone would be a dope not to choose you. A brand runs the breadth and depth of your operation. It flavors everything you do, from the quality of your materials to the way you answer the phones.

A logo? A logo is simply a graphic symbol, containing those same attributes, that identifies them with you.

Some people think that they can just slap a logo on to anything and consider it branded. And don't think those are just little startups. Huge mega-monolithic multinationals do exactly the same thing. But that's not branding. That's called bad marketing and it's another reason why so many bad brands fail.

That's not to say, however, that licensing someone else's logo and slapping it on your product doesn't happen. In fact, if you own a car, washing machine or a VCR, chances are it was built by one of three or four of the world's largest manufacturers, who paste on the logo of whomever pays them to do so. Looked under the hood of your Chevy or Ford lately? Half of those parts are probably Japanese. It's a testament to the power of the Detroit establishment — the rapidly crumbling establishment — that they're still able to rivet their logos to the hood and sell them as Escorts,

Omnis and whatever else they're importing from the east.

But let's get back to you and your logo. How do you effectively use your identity so that it really motivates your targets? Well, here are a couple of pointers:

1 Make sure you have a well-defined, strategically sound brand.

2 Make sure your logo effectively communicates those brand attributes.

3 Make sure that your logo is protectable. In my case, I use the "obnoxious bobbing head in a bubble" graphic, which unless anyone else would be strange enough to want to look like me, is eminently protectable.

4 Once you have the previous three, slap that sucker down on as much real estate as you can tastefully manage. You'll see my bouncing head in the bubble all over the web, and certainly on every page of my site. It's on my business cards, floppy disk labels and practically everything else that can get sprayed with four color ink.

There's a reason for all this, you know, and this is it: when you properly brand your logo, you're creating real value. The kind of value that customers recognize — later on down the line — businesses approach and pay you for. If you're in a service business, that value might be a high-paying endorsement deal. If you're in a product business, that value could avail itself as a manufacturer selling a ton more products because your logo is sitting on their product.

And all this time you thought it was just to look pretty

ACTION ITEMS — CHAPTER EIGHT

1. Decide to change where you eat lunch every Wednesday. Make sure it's something public, like an Italian restaurant that everyone's ignored for the last hundred years.

2. Go there by yourself the first time.

3. Start charting how long it takes until people ask you where you go every Wednesday for lunch.

4. Chart how long it takes until they start asking if they can go with you.

5. Chart how long it takes until someone suggests having the next office party from there.

6. Then, suddenly and for no reason, stop going to the restaurant altogether. Try a Greek place, instead. Repeat as often as necessary

9

SO YOU WANT TO BUILD A WEBSITE

Once you have a brand, stick with it. Once you have a logo, marry it. And once you build a web site, stay the course. One of the biggest mistakes businesses make is gasping for breath in the race to stay current.

One day, I was co-hosting a radio show about online business and technology. As I was doing the curmudgeon schtick that I do, found myself face to face with a veritable antique from the internet world. This was a woman whose site had been up since the Neolithic Age — we're talking early 1990's here — and was running a fairly successful venture promoting artists and their various products.

So we're schmoozing and plugging and bantering along when she hits me with something totally unexpected. Like a bolt from the blue. And this was the comment that caught me completely off guard:

"We're changing our home page design."

SAY WHAT? This woman was no fly-by-night spammoid. She'd been running a successful business for quite a while. Her site wasn't exactly uncomplicated, either. It was a fairly involved design, with artist bio's and samples and cross-links and who knows what else. Most importantly, she was making bucks doing this. So why change it now and risk everything?

Man, that started me thinking about one of the weirdest myths that has become universally accepted by the internet community: changing home page designs.

For some reason — and don't worry, I think I can tell you why — some people out there feel the need to change their home pages more often than you and I change socks. I call these types Net Hamsters, because they keep changing and adding stuff to their home page, hoping that a "fresh" look will somehow maintain their novelty and popularity among the rest of us weary travelers.

Wake up, hamsters. The reality is that unless you have a really, really, really good reason for changing your home page, you're not moving ahead one step. In fact, you're actually doing yourself a major disservice and may even be losing business as a result.

Now before all you neo-post-modern web designers start hurtling java beans at me, let me just explain that I'm not trying to kill your businesses. I know you have to make a buck. But in my humblest of opinions, you should be making your bucks by *designing* web pages, not *re-designing* them. I should be able to drift aimlessly into your studio and tell you all about my business, and you should be able to deliver me a site with a home page that doesn't have to change with the weather. The way you do that is by settling in on a branding strategy for the site *before* you hack one line of code.

The fact is that if you hammer out your brand *before* you start your design, you don't have to constantly update your site, which saves you endless amounts of *dinero* and actually reinforces your brand identity over time.

Right about now, I would expect most of the Net Hamsters to have wrinkled up the fuzzy little noses and retort, "Are you saying that nobody should *ever* change their home page?" To which I reply, Of course not. Calm down. Have a kibble. The point is that very few people really need to change web designs too often, nor should they:

First, if you're in any kind of competitive business, you know that while presenting what you're selling to the public is important, it's the *way* you present it that closes the sale. In effect, your style, layout and home page is every bit the brand image that Kellogg's, Ford and General Electric's corporate identities are. And you don't see them changing their logos every few months "to keep looking fresh", do you?

Well, do you?

Take it from ol' Rob: people want to do business with people who have been around a long time. They want to know that you were there yesterday, you are here today and you'll be there tomorrow. The one entity they *don't* want to entrust their business to is a flighty, honey-do-these-shoes-look-better-with-this-dress kind of enterprise that can't make up its mind what it wants to be, or to whom.

So when should you change your home page? There are a couple of instances that I can think of. If you're delivering timely information, for example, you want the layout to change daily to reflect the image of constantly updated information. Even in those cases, however, the basic format doesn't really change as much as the content.

Another example is when you really have a major shift in your company's marketing direction or services. Let's say you transition from merely reviewing overly-commercial Disney movies to actually offering them for sale through your new secure online system. Hey, that's a substantially new feature set. New functionality. Something that dramatic is well worth a new home page design.

Hell, something that drastic is worth a well-orchestrated public relations campaign.

But if you change you site more often than, say once every 24 months, I'm betting you're a Net Hamster. Running as fast as you can, desperately trying to stay hipper and cooler than the rodent in the next cage and getting nowhere as a result — other than killing your brand equity.

Be smarter than that. Find a design that works. Build your customers' brand loyalty through familiarity, instead of novelty. Otherwise, you may find yourself hopelessly out of breath with nothing more to show for it than a pile of wood shavings.

Frankel's Triangle From Hell

All of the above hardly matters, though, if you don't have your branding strategy locked up and ready to roll before your web builders whip out their first line of HTML code. If you're going to build a Big Brand website, you need to know a few things before you jump in with both feet.

The first thing you should realize is that, like every emerging discipline before it, web development has gone through enough history to have evolved from what it once was. In its Neanderthal days, for example, everything was pretty much text-based, the direct display of coded content that developers pretty much hacked together by hand.. The only real design choice anyone had was using upper or lower case letters.

With the advent of the modern browser, real designers with real graphic files began to invade. Web sites began to take on different looks and personalities. The designer was in charge of the look and feel of the site. The developer was in charge of the "back end" (technical stuff that goes on behind the scenes). And for most of its recent history, that's pretty much where the status of the web development team has stayed.

But no more.

Today, if you hire a team consisting of a designer and a technoid, you're in big trouble. To build a Big Time Brand website, you must meet Frankel's Triangle From Hell:

Welcome to Modern Man's version of the web development team, consisting of equal parts design, technology — and you guessed it — branding. I put branding on the bottom because without it, the other two disciplines have no clear direction as to what to build or how to build it. Lest you take this lightly, let me assure you that it's at this early stage that Big Brand web sites are made or broken.

The first man in has to be the branding guy. He (or she) is the one whose vision is grounded in the eventual profitability of the web site. The tillerman whose steady hand on the rudder keeps the other oarsmen rowing strongly, but more importantly, on course.

The designer incorporates the brand attributes and personality into the site design. The look and feel of the site are only the start of those duties. The site's content, how it gets expressed and the way the end user is supposed to navigate through the site are critical missions. The bars, buttons — everything has to be branded.

Rallying the creative troops

Well-branded design is really, really important if you're serious about doing business on the web. It's the first step toward developing customer loyalty and repeat business. When it comes to web design, the product has to be a consistent creative execution of your brand. Try saying that in front of the mirror a couple of times and see how important it makes you feel. Better yet, try it while wearing a blue pin stripe suit. Works, doesn't it? Well, saying it is one thing, but truly understanding and applying it is what really works.

When you commit to developing a branded website, you're establishing a beachhead on the marketing battlefield, defiantly hoisting your colors and daring the enemy to take their best shot. And if your troops aren't behind you, you're fighting an uphill battle all the way.

The way to get your troops in fighting shape is by articulating your brand to them. Make sure they understand who you are, why you're great and why the world would be foolish not to beat a path to your door. Be accurate, precise and — here's the tough part — make it no more than two sentences long.

After a little hard work — or several years, if you work by committee — you should be able to produce one or two sentences against which all of your buttons, bars and user actions are measured. Then, and only then, are you able to begin working on the site.

But remember, I said that branding is the *consistent* creative execution of your brand. Once you define it, it's got to be everywhere on your site. It's in the way you navigate. The names of your categories. The means by which you present your goods to the public.

The biggest problem you're likely to run into with your designers is the fact that they tend to fall in love with their designs. I know I'll take a lot of yelling for this, but I've just run into it so many times I figure I'd just save you the trouble. The fact is that like great art, great design can be expensive. Not just in terms of money, but in terms of download time, functionality — and ego-driven arguments about style and tastes.

I've been in presentations where designers have rolled out site designs so beautiful they would make Michaelangelo shrink to the back of the room. The only problem is that the designs they created took longer for the average end user to download than it took Mike to paint the Sistine Chapel. Hey, I've got nothing against beauty. I own as many LeRoy Neiman highball glasses as the next guy, but sometimes art has too high a price. Download time can be one of them.

The other nemesis of designers is functionality. I can never understand why some designers don't understand that it's *ease* of use we're going after, not a quest.

Hey, you want to see real obliqueness in action?
Dig this:

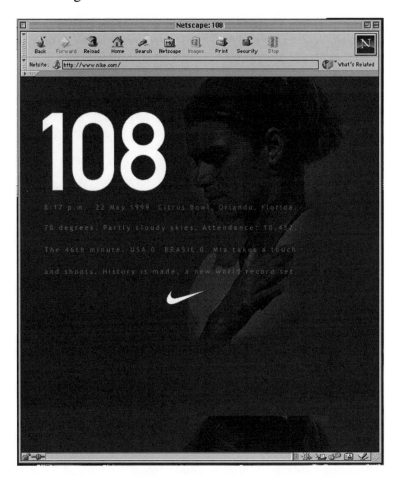

No kidding, this is what *nike.com* looked like the day
I looked it up. I'm sure that this page has some significance
to someone, somewhere. But nobody I know could make
sense of it. For that matter, nobody knew where to click or
why they would even bother looking. And this was put
together by a cutting edge design shop, which just goes to
show you that if you're not careful with design, you may feel
that cutting edge slicing along your throat.

Then again, there's *flycast.com:*

The point is that your creative team is responsible for expressing those traits that resonate from your brand. That's what I like so much about *flycast.com*. Now this is Big Time Branding design. See how they present themselves as a great solution for your advertising problem? More importantly, see how inviting the design is? Accessible, isn't it? No problem figuring out what to click or why to click it.

I know what kind of people I'll be dealing with before I even meet them.

Everything on your site should be developed with your brand in mind. Including the technology that drives it.

Tackling the technoids

One of the fundamental team members of web development is the Technoid. Technical developers are critical to your web success. With one flick of their mouse finger they can bring your entire site down, so a general rule of thumb is to avoid pissing them off whenever possible. Nothing is uglier than the remains of a website at the hands of a vindictive technoid.

Ugh. Horrible.

Although they do have terrific destructive powers, I have tremendous respect for technoids' wonderful creative powers, as well. Not many people realize that the technology that drives the site is often its most creative aspect. They think of technoids as little trolls who sit in dark rooms, scarf fast food and hack code for eighteen hours a day.

They're right, of course, but it's the *way* they sit in dark rooms, scarf fast food and hack code for eighteen hours a day that makes them create the wonderful solutions they produce. Keep in mind that while you and I and the designer can only imagine new ways for end users to interact with our websites, it's the technoids who figure out how to bring our visions into reality. Things as simple as linking or as complex as multi-tiered e-commerce solutions are developed by people who provide the critical link between man machine.

They are indeed fascinating, important people.

But they are *not* gods.

The potential nightmare that can clobber you with technoids is over-engineering. Much like the BMW, where five moving parts do the work of one moving part in a Ford, technoids have a tendency to fall in love with their back-end technology and make things more complex than they need to be. Suppose, for example, that you want people to be able to send you an e-mail message directly from your site. If that's all you want, a simple "mailto" reference in your

HTML will handle that with no problem. On the other hand, a guy who bills by the hour might insist on a scripted program with all kinds of routines that in the end, does the very same thing.

Don't get me wrong. Technoids often contribute the very solutions you seek. But every now and again, a belief in *technology uber alles* sets in, which can delay the entire online development process. The notion that if we just pack the site with one more neat trick, one more new technology that has yet to be adopted by more than four people nationwide, the site will be a killer. That's when you have technoid fever and while there is no cure, it can certainly be arrested, And the way you do that is by keeping your tech team focused on the branding mission.

There should be just enough technology behind the scenes to deliver the brand attributes in the way the brand's personality ought to be delivering them. Nothing more. Nothing less.

If you're heading down the road to build a wholly-integrated, interactive site, you probably need heavy technology, like a dynamic site that serves up pages based on what the end user has asked for. But if yours is a lowly service site (like my own), what the heck do you need all that for? A simple static site is about all you're ever going to need.

Either way, the manner in which your design comes alive and interacts with your end users is just as much a branding statement as the stuff you're hawking for sale. To do the job effectively, you've got to employ all three sides of the Triangle From Hell.

Going with two out of three would be like sitting on a three legged stool that's missing a leg. You could try it, but you'd probably end up on your butt.

ACTION ITEMS — CHAPTER NINE

1. Solicit proposals for your web site from three different design firms.

2. Review each proposal and search for any coherent discussion about brand qualities, specifically, your brand qualities.

3. Look for precise descriptions about how the design will implement and augment those brand strategies.

4. Send each firm a response letter that includes your brand strategy, and request three written examples of how they would implement the strategies on the site.

5. Compare the responses of each firm with their initial proposals.

Repeat the same procedure for your technical and back-end developers.

10

DEMOGRAPHICS AND OTHER GREAT MYTHS

B
eing a branding guy is enough to drive you nuts. One reason why it can make you crazy is that people will ask for advice — and pay decent dollars for it, I might add — only to actually ignore what you tell them.

It's not that these are disagreeable people, mind you. These are simply people who refuse to accept how profoundly the proliferation of media (and the web specifically) has changed marketing and branding strategies. Sure, everyone has their own theories about how to promote their business on the web, but by far, the most wacked-out are the Number Nuts.

At the risk of generating a few hundred thousand poison pen letters, let me explain.

Frankel's First Law of Corporate Motivation clearly states that "90% of the world is driven by fear while the remaining 10% puts fear into the first 90%." Number Nuts fall into the first 90%, who figure that if they bolster their delusional strategies with enough numbers, they won't lose their jobs because they can always blame bad data.

Ah, I can tell by the twinkle in your eye that you can identify at least six, right?

For that reason, most Number Nuts (typically escaped inmates from large ad or media agencies) cling to outmoded techniques like demographics for marketing on the web. Demographics, for those of you unfamiliar with the term, is the practice of dumping people's characteristics into quantifiable categories and then basing your strategy on those numbers. As I mentioned earlier, it could be "white, male mental patients between the ages of 26 and 34." Or "female psychiatrists in the Detroit area over the age of 40." You get the idea.

The problem with demographics is that it worked fine in the days when our choices of media were few and far between. After all, there were, what, maybe three networks for 150 million people in those days. You either watched *Bozo*, reruns of *Fireball 500* or *Bewitched*. Back then, you could pretty well rely on the fact that more guys than girls would be watching *Gunsmoke* at eight o'clock Wednesday evenings and that viewers of the *Lawrence Welk Show* could qualify as certified antiques.

But that's all changed now. At last count, there were at least five television networks in the United States and who knows how many cable channels. There are more radio stations, more magazines than ever before. And the worst part is that media has expanded into people's everyday lives to the point where the lines between entertainment and meaningful data have blurred into a sloppy gray mess.

You and I need to realize that we are witnessing the End of Media Slavery as our fathers and our fathers' fathers knew it. What I'm telling you is that there is now so much choice, so much media, that the traditional mass media model has begun to decompose right before our eyes.

What once was mass media is now media for the masses.

From this day forward, you and I decide what we want to watch along with where and when we want to watch. No more herding us around the tube for a Sunday evening of *The Ed Sullivan Show*. We can videotape it if we want. Or watch it on demand. Or rent it. There are more televisions in more rooms of the house now. No more crowding around the tube or fighting over the remote.

And we haven't even gotten to the web yet.

So what does this have to do with branding, you ask?

Plenty. Mainly that marketing by the numbers worked just fine when the numbers were all that you had. Today, those numbers are crumbling into masses of individuals, each with his or her own tastes, likes and dislikes. The technologies that can deliver your message to those individuals in a cost-efficient manner have finally arrived.

What that means is that the real strategy for your brand on the web is no longer driven by demographics, but by *psychographics*.

Psychographics are way cooler than demo's, because psycho's toss out all that fake number stuff that's really only meant to justify people's jobs. When you go psycho, you don't worry about how many girls in Wisconsin are between the ages of 18 and 24. You get much, much closer to your end-users' brains by murmuring to yourself, "Hmmm, if I want to reach people who enjoy eating chocolate in bed, where would I find them?" As you can see, it's *the desire to consume chocolate* they have in common, not *birthdays*.

The web has at least 40 bazillion channels, each uploading its own show every five nanoseconds viewable at any time of the day. Which means that even members of a well-defined demographic group pursue their own individual interests, whenever and wherever they choose.

Now, perhaps, you might want to take a closer look at Frankel's Prime Directive and see why it's the only strategy that makes sense for brands with any future:

Branding is not about getting your targets to choose you over your competition. Branding is about getting your prospects to see you as the only solution to their problem.

While you're at it, you may want to review Frankel's First Law of Big Time Branding:

Branding is not about you. It's about them.

Weak brands will continue to rely on high mass media awareness, further weakening themselves by ignoring the wants and needs of individual prospects. Big Time Brands, on the other hand, will leverage new media technology and specifically promote their solutions to individuals' problems. The stronger your brand, the better you'll do.

It's The Revenge of Brand X and — once again — *that's* where we're all headed, whether the pundits like it or not.

That's the reason why I almost always recommend choosing psychographics over demographics on the web. Oh, the Number Nuts will still try to dazzle you with all sorts of numbers. But believe me, only one number that really counts: your bottom line. And if you think it counts a lot in the offline world, just wait a few paragraphs until you see how absolutely critical lit is online.

Psychographics Drive the Web

There's no question that branding your business is the key to your long term success, both online and offline. But a really solid, healthy brand brings them in and keeps them coming back for more — especially on the web. That's because the web's architecture is niche-based.

No, it's more than that.

It's niche critical. In fact, Frankel's First Law of Web Branding states:

The more niche, the better you do.

The web is the first medium in the history of the known universe that actually rewards you for being narrow-minded. The reason for that is pretty simple when you nut it out: Every other medium previously enjoyed and corrupted by semi-intelligent beings worked on the notion of mass media. The thinking was that if you sprayed enough people at one time with one message, a certain percentage of them would find the message motivating enough to actually drive down to your store and flash their credit card. It worked fabulously for the printing press. Newspapers and magazines trumpeted their circulation numbers right up there on page one for everyone — including potential advertisers — to see. The minute radio and TV hit the airwaves, it was pretty much the same thing with viewership ratings. All over the world, careers sky-rocketed and plummeted based entirely on who was watching, reading or listening to what. Every advertiser completely bought into the notion of mass media.

Even the post office got into the act, with direct mail marketing strategies. Today, people still gage their mass media's effectiveness based on the old rule of thumb that "a 1% response" is the threshold a campaign must break to be considered successful. Of course, if you despise rules of thumb as much as I do, that actually translates into *if you waste less than 99% of your resources, you're considered successful.*

The point, of course, is that mass media has been really great to us. It's brought us advancement in technology, rapid dissemination of information and endless reruns of *Get Smart*. The good lord only knows how many *Veg-O-Matics* and *Abdominizers* have been sold through the tube alone, based on the mass media model over the last century, so it's only natural that the same folks who flood the airwaves with infomercials hawking electric forks would want to port their strategies over to the next mass medium: the web.

Unfortunately, it doesn't work that way, because the web is so niche-critical. And the reason the web is so niche-critical is that it's the first medium to deliver its mass messages to its users according to their individual schedules, instead of its own. Whereas television, radio and print all tell you when, where and in which edition to find your interest, the web works completely differently. The web is built on the concept of delivering what you want, whenever you want it. More importantly, the web is driven by people *who already know what they want*, looking for a place where they can buy it. That's why they type in keywords at search engines. And the more precise you are about asking for whatever it is you want, the quicker and higher quality result you get.

Imagine watching television like that. No TV guide. No VCR Plus. Just a quick tap of the keyboard instructing the tube that you not only wanted to watch an episode of *The Donna Reed Show*, but the specific episode where Shelly Fabares attempts to launch her singing career by crooning *Johnny Angel.*

Can you say *psychographically-driven*?

Well, that's exactly how it happens on the web. Users may tell a search engine, for example, exactly what they want and within a heartbeat, they're presented with a list of choices that match their choice criteria as closely as possible. Naturally, the more vague the user's choice criteria, the broader the range of choices presented, which literally throws up a half million or more useless links to irrelevant websites.

They may get their leads from user groups, e-mail lists, site links – whatever special interest associations they enjoy and that power the web.

Taking all of that into consideration, you can now understand why it only takes about five or six minutes for even the newest of users wrestling with a search engine to learn how to define — or more appropriately, *narrow* — their searches as specifically as possible. They want what *they* want, not what someone else thinks they want.

And that represents two huge opportunities for you.

First, if you remember how finely the users tune their

searches, you can be fairly sure that if they actually find something that fits their request, they're going to become incredibly high-probability prospects. Second, you may want to think about who's going to top the list of the items returned by those search engines. If the phrase "well-branded companies" jump to mind, you're on the right track. Because the search engine, driven by the users' criteria, places the most accurate matches at the top of the list. And the most accurate matches tend to be those whose sites are well-defined, with content containing more of the relevant keywords in their natural context.

So why would I bring this up right here and now? Good question.

Offline Pegs and Online Holes

The reason I bring this up to you is that if you have any plans to launch a brand on the web, you'd be well-advised to market it there, as well. You'd be even better advised to mix your marketing strategy with a balance of offline media. But you'd go straight to hell in a hand basket if you followed the advice of some of the world's leading media brains and attempted to port your offline media strategies to your online efforts.

Unfortunately, that's exactly what some of the world's largest companies are doing. They buy their web marketing media the same exact way they buy their offline TV, print and radio — and then sit there scratching the heads wondering why the damn thing doesn't work. Next thing you know, you read some knucklehead in the *Wall Street Journal* ranting about how "the web isn't living up to its promise".

The key realization is that the web isn't at all like television, print or radio. Yes, it does reach a massive audience and it does deliver text, sound and motion. But that's about where the similarities end. The web is global. It's unregulated. And best of all, it allows anyone to contribute whatever content may be of interest to anyone else, owing to the fact that, unlike any other medium before it, its physical proportions are infinite. While TV and radio stations are limited to the 24 hour day and printed publications are walled in by the dimensions of a printed page, the web exists as zillions of bits and bytes, fragmented throughout the world on an ever-increasing number of computer hard drives. No limit on inventory means that content drives value, instead of scarcity. The low cost of entry means that the number of "channels" available for viewing can double every month. And so on.

When you drink all of that data in, you begin to understand how freedom of choice, coupled with individual empowerment, gives rise to a totally different culture around the web than you find with traditional offline media. And that's why a Big Time Brand is so damn critical to your success. For the first time in the mass medium age, nobody can tell anyone else what to watch or when to watch it. It's all done by user choice — psychographics again — and that means brand loyalty plays a much bigger part in the equation.

Web users love freedom. A whole new culture has sprung up around it, affecting everything from the value of content to the way in which the users interact with it.

And that's why so many offline disciplines simply don't work online.

That having been said, I thought it would be wise to explode a few other myths that simply won't make the leap from hyperspace to cyberspace.

Ad brokers: Who's zooming whom?

I just love all these clowns who do whatever they can to make their lives easier. There's certainly no quicker way to grind your business into the floor than seeking out the most convenient solution. And for my money ad brokering services are the best at that.

One reason why I can't stand ad brokers is that they seem to think that branding and advertising are the same thing. That somehow, if you expose your logo to enough people over a period of time, you have indeed established your brand.

You haven't of course. What you've more likely established are the grounds for your getting fired. Because while advertising does raise the awareness of a brand, it never does the job of branding itself. Branding occurs long before the first ads ever are run up the flagpole to send corporate yes-men clucking with delight.

Nevertheless, a substantial industry has grown up overnight on the web, determined to part you with your money by brokering and/or selling ad space on the internet. It was a sucker's paradise from the beginning: after all, if thousands of web sites are springing up every day, how do you really know where you should advertise your business? Which are the best? And how do you really know?

The answer is fairly simple. You don't. And neither does anyone else. But that doesn't mean people won't try to sell you their expertise.

Most ad brokers weren't even in the business a few years ago. Press them really hard, and most won't be able to tell you the difference between a demographic and a psychographic. What they will tell you are buzzwords that have little, if any, real impact on growing your business.

They'll explain the concept of Cost Per Thousand impressions (CPM's) and Click Through Rates (CTR's) along with a bevy of other acronyms borrowed mainly from offline media departments. What they don't tell you is that all of these metrics are measurements of media purchasing and have little to do with branding, or marketing for that matter. The reason I bring this up is because ad brokers are just one more instance of convenient solutions that don't really work or necessarily address your problems.

Two things bother me about ad brokers and both of them are serious: first, most aren't in business for themselves, the way you are. Fact is, most of them have been on the web for about five minutes more than you have. But their techno-phrases and official-sounding numbers are comforting. It sounds like they know what they're talking about, and since nobody knows enough to call them on it, most neophytes buy into it.

The second issue I have with ad brokers is that most often, the brokers you meet aren't *buying* space on your behalf, they're *selling* space on their clients' behalf. Read that last sentence again, rub your eyes and believe it: these guys don't represent you. They represent the sites that have advertising space to sell. Which means that they have no incentive to show you what's best for your business. In fact, your business doesn't figure into the equation at all, save for its ability to pay its bills.

My point isn't to trash ad brokers, incidentally. It's to warn you against convenient solutions that ring of familiarity. Advertising on the web isn't the same thing as offline promotion. The tools and dynamics are different. And anyone who can't explain that to you isn't worth a return phone call. These are the same people who will tell you that branding on the web doesn't work — when it's probably the most effective tool you've got. They're going to sell you what they've got to sell. They'll sell what they know. They'll sell what's convenient — not what's in your best interests.

Working the web isn't as difficult as people try to make it seem. But it is different. So the best advice I can give you is to accept it: you're not in Kansas anymore. This is a new ball game, with its own rules and customs. Better you should learn the territory than get lost in it.

Ad agencies: No branding here.

While ad brokers are busy trying to sell you space on someone else's websites, ad agencies are trying to convince you they know what to put there. Trust me on this: ad agencies are the very last places to find out how to brand yourself on the web. There are about a thousand reasons I can give you as to why that is, but let's take these for starters:

1 **Ad agencies are overly in-bred.** It's true. Filled with people who are hopelessly out of touch with reality, most agencies are staffed with people who have little or no real business experience. No worries about the bottom line. Consequently, the work they produce tends to be based more on promoting awareness rather than substantive marketing strategy. These are art school majors. Unpublished novelists and screenwriters. Sure, they may throw in an MBA or two in a really nice suit, but you have no idea how rough those guys have it. All those years in grad school just to put up with film students who can't coordinate bad eyewear with strange clothes.

2 **Ad agencies are hopeless followers.** Before 1970, advertising shaped the trends and opinions of the consuming public. Then lawyers and accountants took over the world and the industry that used to challenge and vitalize the world quietly rolled over and died. The industry became the first to do nothing and the second to do everything. Latching on to trends or over-budgeting media buys took the place of smart strategies and stimulating executions. As a result, an entire generation of ad people have grown up thinking that advertising is really just about hitching a ride on the latest trend, instead of launching it. If that's what you want for your business, by all means, go ahead. But realize that anything new actually frightens ad people today — especially the web. They don't know it. They don't understand

it. But they won't admit it. Instead, they'll try to sell you their converted offline models and bring in a consultant to shore up their lack of knowledge.

3 **Ad agencies know little, if anything, about branding.** I can't really fault them for this, though, because branding isn't really their job. It's yours. Your brand should be fully developed before you even think about advertising, because the agency's job is really to increase awareness of that brand. Of course, being ad people, they'll tell you they're perfectly capable of cultivating your brand — but then, they'll also offer to wash your car for you, too, if you ask nicely.

Metrics mean nothing

A few paragraphs ago, I mentioned CPM's and CTR's. I don't know why marketing people love these acronyms so much. Maybe it's because it makes them sound like they know what they're talking about. But increasingly, you're going to find that these mega-metrics have little, if anything, to do with developing your business.

CPM's are especially guilty of this. Measuring the cost per thousand visitors to a site is preposterously based on the offline notion that the web really is television dressed in computer clothing. It's not. The web is about individual access, not global manipulation, so all those old tactics and measurements simply don't work. If you don't believe me, try this:

Which would you rather get: a 1% response rate from a million ad impressions or a 10% response rate from 400,000? It doesn't take an Einstein to figure out that by focusing on a smaller — but more responsive — target, your return on investment can skyrocket. But if you compare the CPM's, you're likely to find that even at the same budget levels, the million-man purchase has a lower CPM — and is likely to be recommended by a "media expert" who has no alternative to his old offline strategies. Meanwhile, you're paying up the wazoo for an incredible 99% waste factor on a budget that is quite likely larger than the 100,000 buy.

The same myth occurs with click through rates, too, where people with no other means of generating traffic try to convince you that clicking on banners is the way to get people to buy from you.

Well, it's not.

I'm here to tell you that the way to build a solid business is by building a solid brand. Because people rely on good brands. They flock to great ones. And in a medium like the web — where people come looking for you — that's the magic bullet.

ACTION ITEMS — CHAPTER TEN

1. Try to describe a typical chocolate lover *demographically.*

2. Try to get one or more advertising agencies or ad brokers to do it.

3. If they do it, have them recommend three websites that cater to that demographic.

4. Try to describe a typical chocolate lover *psychographically.*

5. Try to find three websites that cater to that psychographic (hint: try typing in the keyword "chocolate" at *Yahoo.com, AltaVista.com or Google.com.*)
Identify your traffic needs as either a high-volume or high-quality.

6. Practice explaining to people why CPM's have little relevance on the web.

11

THE GOOD, THE BAD AND THE WORTHLESS

S till think that this is all theory, eh? That old Rob is all hat and no cattle? Fine. I don't blame you. If I shelled out a few bits for this book I'd want some real data, too. So let's take a little stroll down the internet and see exactly what kind of brands are out there.

A word of warning before we go, however.

First, this book is nailed down in time by the permanence of ink and paper. Nothing I can do about it, except to warn you that the pages you're about to view may not be online by the time you read this, It doesn't matter, though. Because I'm out to show you a the good, the bad and the worthless when it comes to online branding. It's not my intention to dump on any of them, but as you'll see, there's obviously a lot of room for improvement in most cases. So let's just chalk it up to a free consultation on my part, free publicity for these sites and a real-life experience for you.

Not that I favor one approach over another, but let's start out with the ones that, shall we say, could use the most improvement.

The Bad

By now, it should be clear to you that the very worst thing you can do branding on the web or anywhere else, is sit there spouting off how terrifically wonderful you are. It may annoy people in the offline world, but online, it whips them up into a downright frenzy of hostility. I mean, when you think about it, what has Bill Gates ever done to you except make your life easier? He essentially standardized the PC and its operating system, making software and hardware cheaper for anyone whoever touched a keyboard and he's *still* among the most hated guy in America.

Why?

Not because he wears glasses and not because every day is a bad hair day. It's because Bill Gates and Microsoft carry themselves with a brazen-yet-unspoken aloofness. While they may pay lip service to their end users, the truer, underlying agenda is never more than one angstrom below the surface:

We're big. We're dominant. *Play ball with us or we'll kill you.*

And so while this may be a bit extreme, is sure does go a long way toward showing you how incredibly uncon-cerned a business can be when it comes to projecting their brand. On the web, this kind of branding is classified as a felony, requiring an immediate, if not mandatory, outright rejection from people whose culture is based on sharing, empowerment and niceness.

Of course, not everyone is that blatant. But most are that uninterested. Take a look at what Procter & Gamble was up to at the time this book was written:

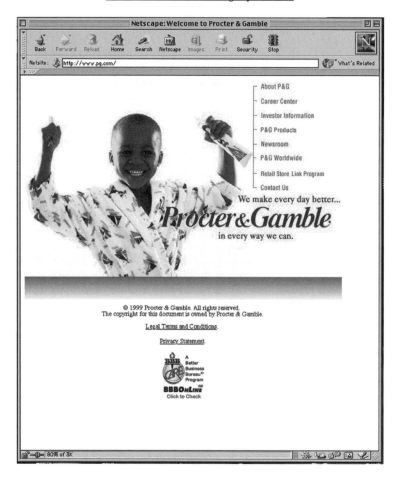

This, ladies and gentlemen, is the best that a multi-billion dollar staple of the American economy could produce on a budget that surely exceeded both your and my combined annual incomes. Here is Procter & Gamble ostensibly claiming to "make every day better in every way we can," yet check out the various sections of the site that supposedly are there to deliver on that promise:

> **About P&G:** Okay, I can live with that. Maybe I want to know about the company and how it manages its business. A little about its history. An anecdote or two about some of its products. I can accept a corporate belch here.

Career Center: I know that P&G needs people but is that the second most important issue they have to explore with their end users? Bear in mind that this is a public site, not a business-to-business operation.

Investor Information: Excuse me, but isn't this the place that makes the soaps and detergents and stuff like that? Where are the household brands that I'm interested in? Why am I here?

Newsroom: Anyone want to take bets on what the story items in this section concern themselves with? More about me. Nothing about you. An exercise in ivory tower-ism that achieves near championship form.

P&G Worldwide: More about us! Only now it's more about us around the whole world. What about you, the people whose hard-earned money made us the mega-billion juggernaut that we are today? Nothing.

Retail Store Link Program: Fabulous. Listings of places that feature more about us. Thrilling. Captivating, isn't it?

Contact Us: Click here to e-mail your comments — about what? What a great shot you took of that little kid in his bathrobe?

Clearly, Procter & Gamble had no idea — and cared even less — about understanding the community it decided to invade with its web site. Take a close look at this home page and you'll see the ultimate in Branding Crime: saying something, meaning nothing and delivering even less.

P&G would have been much better off with a Big Time Brand strategy. Can you imagine a link that allowed end-users to trade tips and tricks for toothpaste? How to get your kids to brush their teeth? How to save even more on Crest by buying it direct? Why mouthwash finishes the job that brushing only starts? What about a directory of dentists that belong to that ridiculous American Dental Association?

And that's just the stuff they could begin doing with

toothpaste. At last count, Procter & Gamble had a bazillion different brands for the household. They have the world marching to their website — and the best they can do is come up with eight irrelevant links and a kid in a bathrobe, flanked by a tagline that means absolutely nothing to anyone: *We make every day better in every way we can?* Well, who doesn't? Drug dealers and hijackers don't like to have bad days, either. Is there any way that line can be any more vague?

And maybe that's a good place to take a little detour.

Saying something, Meaning Nothing

Ever look at an ad and scratch your head, wondering what the heck these people were trying to sell you? I get that way all the time. Probably because I'm old.

Nah.

Why mince words? Probably because they're *stupid*. In fact, if you look around a little, you'll find that while lots of people enjoy talking, very few of them actually say anything. The state of communication has disintegrated to the point where people say what *sounds* right, instead of delivering a clearly thought message.

Think about it. Advertising tag lines like "Just do it", "Some people just know how to fly", "A different kind of car company" may sound like they mean something, but when examined closely, mean nothing at all. I mean, you could apply those lines to any competitors in their fields and they'd be just as effective.

Or ineffective, if you get my drift.

Admittedly, the most egregious offenders of these sensibilities are those inbred creative people at traditional ad agencies. People who feel that weird hair and strange eye wear compensate for their lack of marketing and communication skills. But remember that those kids have one thing you probably don't:

A huge advertising budget.

They don't have to be clear, because they've got the money to hammer you over the head with the same coded message a bazillion times and sponsor every special interest event from tennis to tiddly winks.

The smaller your budget is, the clearer your message has to be, because it has to work faster. Who's got time to figure out some oblique Freudian reference when all you really want to do is sell more staplers?

This is why you should always put clarity before creativity, in virtually all your communications to your staff, your customers — heck, even your wife. Enhancing clarity of communication shortens sales cycles, makes communications more appealing, amplifies management techniques and provides more rewarding social relationships.

It can also save you big money.

Lack of clarity costs businesses millions of dollars annually in unclear memos, minutes, correspondence, advertising — and branding. Think I'm kidding? How many times have you had *this* conversation:

> YOU: Hey, Bobby! What's shakin'?
> BOBBY: Aw, you know. The same old same old...What about you?
> YOU: You kiddin' me? It's been the same for me most of this year!
> BOBBY: Really? What's keeping you so busy?
> YOU: Well, it's the same old stuff, only more of it. You know how it is...
> BOBBY: Tell me about it. You still seeing what's her name?
> YOU: Wow, it really *has* been a while since I talked to you!
> BOBBY: Forever, man.
> YOU: So what are you doing lately?
> BOBBY: I've got a couple of new things I'm trying, but basically waiting to.....

What, exactly, have you learned from that exchange?

This could go on forever and nothing would *ever* be communicated. And that's the state of communications today. Heck, even the most popular TV shows are reruns and retrospectives of past lives we all once lived. Nobody believes commercials anymore. In fact, nobody believes anyone anymore. And why should they? We've become victims of language inflation, where words have lost all their value.

Still think the big boys have all the smarts? Take a look at these taglines offered up by some of America's biggest — and supposedly brightest — companies over the last few years. See if you can tell who they are, what they do and why they're the best solution for your needs. The answers are located in Appendix B:

Tagline/Brand Positioning	Company	Meaning
We answer to the world.		
Just do it.		
Rising.		
Let's make things better.		
Is it in you?		
The dot in "dot com"		
Long live sport.		
Just imagine.		
It's time for clarity.		
Always.		

So why I am I ranting this way?

Because part of branding is separating yourself from the clutter. And if you can communicate clearly and precisely — the first time — guess who's going to get to the hearts and minds of your prospects faster?

Yup.

Hit 'em hard. Hit 'em fast. But make sure it's a clearly communicated shot. In the world of amateur gibberish, you'll stand out like a sore thumb — all the way to the bank.

Now do you understand why it's not a question of

money? Are we having fun yet? Let's take a look at another:

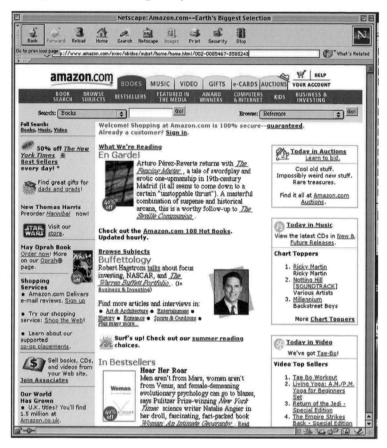

This is *amazon.com*. The IPO darling of the internet. The stuff legends are made of. And hopefully, a major distributor of this book. Look hard. Look long. And tell me if there's anything here that will keep you from clicking over to *barnesandnoble.com*. Anything?

Nothing.

Hey, I'm not looking to win any popularity contests, but surely it doesn't take rocket scientist to figure out that there's not much in Amazon's program to promote any kind of brand value or loyalty to its end users. Sure, they practically invented the profitable Affiliate Program — and did invent one-click ordering — but what do you think is going to happen the day *barnesandnoble.com* figures out that affiliates sell their loyalty to the highest bidder? Or engineers their way around the one-click thing?

Amazon gets sold down the river, so to speak.

The Good

And now, for something completely different: a company that gets it:

You just gotta love Federal Express. Well, *you* may

not, but I certainly do, because they understand what Big Time Branding is all about. The beauty of this site is its consistency and credibility of brand. The entire site is a solution for end users. Unlike Procter & Gamble, FedEx spends about 99% of its home page empowering its end users and 1% on itself. In fact, you have to really hunt down the teeny-weeny little link that whisks you off to other "FDX Companies."

The first thing you notice about this site is that it's chock full of ways to make you do whatever you do that much better and faster. And FedEx goes way beyond the call of duty, by offering you all kinds of services and tools that they really don't have to. I mean, the core business here is getting your package from one place to another. But FedEx does more than that:

> You can notify them to ship your package — a timesaver!
> Type up a shipping bill and print it out on your laser printer.
> Track it from the site — a career saver!
> Find the nearest drop off location — another timesaver!
> Search for stuff — how convenient!
> Utilize more business tools for FREE that THEY developed at THEIR cost!

And to top it all off, the FedEx people are slick enough to know that not everyone has a giant 20 inch monitor crowding out the desk. See how they designed their home page so that it fits a smaller monitor without requiring you to scroll all around? That's a beautiful example of sub-textual communication. Real credibility. It's FedEx telling the us poor schnooks, "Hey, we know not everyone can afford state of the art stuff. We're here to help you any way we can — even if it means downsizing the dimensions of our home page."

Barely a mention of how fabulous they are.

Now hang that up right next to our toothpaste merchants: is there any comparison as to which one cultivates the greater loyalty? I think not.

Big Time Branding, Small Time Budget

Okay, I'll admit it. I have a soft spot in my heart for start-ups and small businesses. I always root for the underdog. Mainly because I grew up a small kid, believing in brains over brawn. It worked for me then and it works for small businesses now, because it doesn't take a huge amount of money to develop an incredibly strong Big Time Brand.

And this is the part where I get to prove it.

Take a look at this small business site.

How much do you suppose *supremevideo.com* invested here? I can't nail it to the penny, but I can pretty much guarantee it doesn't come close to what Procter & Gamble spent for *pg.com*. I like this site. Not because it's particularly beautiful or that I think its URL is wonderfully inspired. No, I like this site because the owners intuitively understand the notion of a Big Time Brand. The way you can tell is by the way they've approached their task.

If there's anything the web doesn't need, it's another bargain basement for consumer electronics. You know that. I know that. And it's a pretty safe bet that these guys knew what they were getting into, too. Knowing that a dependency on lowest price was the signature on their death warrant, these guys played it smart. Instead of promising the lowest price (itself a totally non-believable claim) they promised a better value at a reasonably low price.

"The right price. The right advice"

Hey, it's not an award-winner, but it sure brings home the bacon.

By giving customer service equal billing with low price, supremevideo.com came up with a strong believable brand . A fair trade off that a consumer could buy into. A proposition that's so clearly articulated you can almost hear one consumer referring it to another:

Well, their price wasn't the lowest, but those guys were so helpful, it was really worth the few extra bucks .

They don't even display prices next to the items they feature, suggesting that this brand really does place knowledge and quality way over price. That quality is truly more important than price. What *supremevideo.com* does is move their commodities off of price point. They not only promise it in their brand; they deliver it on their site.

Take a gander at that side bar. See any bragging? Any chest-beating? Nope. But what you do see is the stuff of Big Time Brands: all the information you can eat about VCR's, DVD's and whatever else tickles your electronic fancy, plus a couple of niceties that any consumer would welcome; a newsletter, an invitation to contact them, a search function and the ever-popular money-saving special.

Could they push it further? Sure. And one day they probably will. But for now, what you're witnessing is the birth of a baby Big Time Brand that wasn't born with a silver spoon in its mouth.

Big Time Budget, Big Time Brand

Don't get me wrong. I'm not against spending money if you got it. It's just that there's so much money being dumped into poorly branded sites that I could, well, write a book about it. But every so often, a big bucks site makes it on to the web that gives me hope. And one of the best examples I can find of that is *nytimes.com*, the web site for the *New York Times*.

What qualifies this site as a Big Time Brand is so subtle that you almost miss it. Take a look at this home page. Notice anything missing? I'll tell you if you can't:

No overly-intrusive banners. The editorial still rules over the advertising. So why does that make nytimes.com a Big Time Brand? Well, there are a couple of reasons:

First, the folks at the *New York Times* were smart enough to build a solid brand offline, to start with. Over the course of the last three ice ages, the *New York Times* has been known as one of the finest journalistic publications in the country.

Or if you're from New York, the finest journalistic publication in the world.

Either way, they knew their mission was to port as much of that brand value to the web as possible, keeping as much of the brand's integrity intact as possible. That accounts for the page's faithful adaptation of layout and content.

For all intents and purposes, it really does look the way you'd imagine an "online newspaper" to look.

More importantly, the *New York Times* team understood that it was developing its site for its readers, not for itself. As such, they took their end-users' psychographical values into account when they laid it all out. So even though this site could rake in a hefty rate for banners on its front page, the *New York Times* people have both class and common sense: know that *New York Times* readers would never stand for such an outrage and promptly dump the site from their browsers' bookmark files.

Of course, you don't see it until it's pointed out, but it's there, alright. Want to see another viewpoint? Feast your baby blues on what the *Los Angeles Times* has to offer with *latimes.com* and see if the difference is still so subtle:

Whoa, stop the bus!

On the same page that I want to understand the world's heaviest issues, I can win a used Buick! Somewhere to the right of a masthead that bears almost no resemblance to the city's leading paper, I can click and be taken to an antique dealer's studio! Hey, is this serious journalism, or what?

Clearly, the *Los Angeles Times* had no intention of

maintaining its legacy or promoting its heritage when it launched this baby. Bear in mind that the *Times* is the country's largest metropolitan newspaper. A big wheel in the nation's second largest city. And even with all that, whatever franchise they might have brought with them to the web was left out on the front porch to rot in the rain.

What the *Los Angeles Times* neglected in this site pales in comparison to *whom* they neglected: their offline readers. Where *nytimes.com* is designed its site around its brand qualities that its readers cherish most, *latimes.com* never even gives its readers a passing nod. And that's the ultimate difference: *nytimes.com* is about the people of New York; *latimes.com* is about the *Los Angeles Times*.

But it doesn't stop there.

At the time of this writing, the *Los Angeles Times* was also engaged in the practice of charging for articles users retrieved from its archives, even though many other publications freely give theirs away. Talk about a disincentive to end users. Is there anything that turns readers loyalties around faster than charging them for something they can get a million other places for free?

Yeesh.

Can a situation like that get any worse, you ask? Unfortunately, yes. But you wouldn't believe it if I simply wrote about it. So here it is for you to see for yourself.

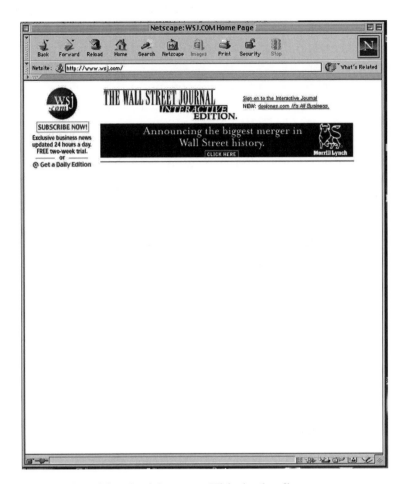

Yes, friends, it's true. This is the first stop on your way to *wsj.com*, the digital home of the *Wall Street Journal*. And if you don't pay their admission, this is as far as you get. That's right, *wsj.com*, owners of what is possibly the planet's foremost financial brand, kill off a substantial amount of that brand's goodwill simply by making the site a pay-to-play proposition.

I could be wrong, but from where I sit, this is a simply fabulous way to kill your brand on the web. After all, accurate financial information isn't exactly tough to find on the web. Neither is financial analysis and advice. So what does *wsj.com* hope to accomplish by restricting access to its site other than communicating to the world its profound misunderstanding of web culture of shared knowledge and empowerment?

Clearly, neither *latimes.com* nor *wsj.com* understand the underlying fundamentals of Big Time Branding, which is clearly stated in Frankel's First Law:

It's not about you. It's about them.

And if you don't develop your brand for them, believe me, they'll click to another brand that does.

ACTION ITEMS — CHAPTER ELEVEN

1. List five of your favorite major brands

2. Grab a brochure from each one of them

3. Grab an ad from each one of them.

4. Go to the web site of each one of them.

5. Which ones manage to port their brands consistently from offline to online?

6. Now do the same thing for your company. How does it fare?

12

WHEN GOOD BRANDS GO BAD: 10 THAT COULD DO BETTER

Acertain number of people will yank my lapel at any given event, asking me how I could possibly say that this brand or that brand isn't a good brand. After all, they reason, if Coca-Cola is such a lousy brand, how come something like one percent of the entire globe be consuming their products?

The answer I give them is found in the question. Sure, there are successful brands. But you don't have to search too terribly far and wide to find mediocrity rising to the top. Heck, just try holding a coherent conversation with any movie or television executive and you'll find that intelligence, skill and talent have less to do with success than having a father in the business. Luck, circumstances, sales tactics, bribery — call it what you will — often determine the success of a business.

But they don't determine the success of a brand.

To prove my point, here are ten major league brands that, in my humble opinion, could have been branded a whole lot better:

1 **Amazon.com:** Yes, they're everyone's cyberdarling, but the truth of the matter is that nobody holds one ounce of allegiance to Amazon. And why should they? To this date, Amazon has ridden on the coattails of the internet revolution, surfing the rising awareness of the web itself by becoming everyone's illustration of e-commerce on the web. There was a time when you couldn't even utter the phrase "e-commerce" without some screen flashing a picture of the web site, as if it were the one and only site in the world to ever charge people money.

Throughout the years, however, Amazon hasn't developed any brand value at all. Its main advertising message continues to focus on its vast inventory, which leaves it vulnerable to any and all pretenders to the throne. They should have more outreach, more book-oriented programs. Something. Anything. If Amazon were truly different than other bookstores — online or off — they should have said so by now. But they haven't, and if they don't, they'll soon have transformed themselves into nothing more than a holding company for their other ventures. I'd even lay odds that within the next decade, books will be a small fraction of their business — through shrinkage, not growth. After all, if you can't think of a reason to stay loyal to Amazon, chances are not many others out there can, either.

Think it can't happen? Anyone remember Osborne computers?

Big Time Solution: Even if you took their book business by itself — as it should, considering its their highest awareness business — Amazon should stop with the "lumbering giant" image and start offering the ancillary services that empower its patrons. Programs should serve to strengthen their position in the book universe, like special interest groups that spawn real, live terrestrial discussion groups, alliances with brand-compatible partners like Starbucks would do them well. Being all things to all people risks being nothing to anyone.

2 Prodigy Business Services: Poor old Prodigy, the bastard offspring of that one-nighter between Sears and IBM, now cast out to scrape by on the crumbs and scraps that AOL won't touch. If I were the emotional type, I'd cry my heart out for Prodigy Online Services. But I'm far more practical than that. The mere fact that Prodigy is still in business after years of inept management is almost enough to make me believe in miracles. It truly is a testament to grit and determination.

Or maybe just stupidity, I don't know.

What I do know is that as recently as 1999, Prodigy was staged for a comeback with Prodigy Business Services. They were lining up the whole shooting match, including a moderately successful IPO that even managed to stop the media's laughing long enough to report the story. Market conditions at the time were ripe for e-commerce and the rise of the micro-business class was just beginning to swell its ranks. Prodigy was boasting that its new service was going to cater to that class.

If there ever was a fastball down the center of the plate, this was Prodigy's chance. They could have taken their place in the sun, because all the other national brands' beach chairs were already taken: AOL was for simpletons, CompuServe was for serious businesses. What else was left? AT&T? Earthlink?

So what do they do? Nothing.

Perfectly poised to capture the market that everyone knows is there but nobody knows how to capture, Prodigy's products — anemic though they are — could have helped to branded themselves as the online service that empowers micro-businesses. Moms and Pops the world over would have logged on and sworn by the service that was created and customized just for their needs.

But they didn't. And probably won't. Hope you didn't buy the stock.

Big Time Solution: Prodigy should dump their entire general focus and invest big time into the online world of Mom and Pop e-commerce. Instead of merely supplying tools and charging for them, they should foster a community among their users to increase each others' businesses and alliances therein (see *FrankelBiz*).

3 **Nissan**: When Nissan first invaded America, they weren't known as Nissan. They were called Datsun and they were a Big Time Brand. I suppose you had to be there, but when Datsun arrived on the scene, American consumers had one thought on their minds: how were they ever going to afford gasoline again?

Aside from Elton John and David Bowie, the mid 1970's are perhaps most famous for that famous fraudulent fiasco we all knew as the Arab oil embargo. Somehow, the American press bought the story that despite the United States' ability to crank out more crude oil than almost any other nation on the planet, our "dependence on foreign oil" caused prices to punch through the ceiling. People waited in lines for hours. For a while, there was even a schedule for when you could buy gas. You were either an "even" day or an "odd" day buyer.

It was, in a word, laughable. Inconvenient, yes, but laughable.

Sensing this climate, Datsun introduced its line of lighter, cheaper — formerly known as "flimsy" — cars as "fuel-efficient" vehicles. And for the next ten years or so, sold their fleet with the tag, "Datsun saves." It was profoundly effective. What a brand. Anyone who wanted to save gas didn't even *think* about an American car. They raced right past the Ford and Chevy showrooms and loaded up with Datsuns.

The brand was so strong, in fact, that a decade later, when some moron at Nissan (Datsun's parent company in Japan) decided to change Datsun's name to Nissan for consistency's sake, people kept calling them Datsuns for years after.

Today, Nissan's mindshare is down — way down — from where it was in its earliest Datsun days. And no wonder. There's no reason to remember what a Nissan is or why you should buy one. It was real brand *hara-kiri*.

Big Time Solution: Now that the oil shortage myth has been dispelled, Nissan should become a specialist in optimal performance vehicles. They should stress that their sports cars are designed by entirely different divisions than the guys who design their light utility vehicles, all of whom are motivated by a strong allegiance to an Eastern ideal of excellence.

4 Kodak: Weep for this one, folks. After dominating the world's imagery for a thousand years, Kodak's empire began crumbling in the late 1980's and hasn't stopped yet. Fuji has eaten their lunch. Some of it due to aggressive sales tactics, to be sure. But a stronger brand would have protected Kodak if they hadn't been so successful for such a long time.

Sitting back on their fat cash reserves, Kodak must have thought that the digital revolution was just a fluke. The same kind of thinking that dismissed Elvis and rock and roll as nothing more than a passing fad. What they forgot to tell the kids in Rochester is that Elvis earns more dead than he ever did while he was alive.

While Kodak flounders around for a life preserver, trying to be all things to everyone, they're missing the boat completely. If they don't get their act together soon, even their massive inertia won't be enough to stop the bleeding.

Big Time Solution: Kodak doesn't need a focus group to tell them what their main liabilities and assets are. You and I know them. Kodak's legacy has always been quality imaging. Their big mistake was focusing that quality imaging aspect on paper coated with silver nitrate. Instead of laying back and watching where the market goes, Kodak should be positioning itself as an imaging innovator — God only knows it can afford to make mistakes that its lesser counterparts can't. Kodak should be following up that innovation with programs and cultures that invite participation from developers and end-user — and doing it in a much more public way.

5 **McDonald's:** Someone has to wake up the fallen arches, a once-great company with a bullet-proof brand that's decayed into the wallpaper of the fast food world. It's painful to watch a former champion limp blindly along the boulevard, telling anyone who will listen how great he once was.

At one time, McDonald's was unbeatable. You knew who they were and why you went there. The food was cheap, fast and convenient — end of story. Then someone got some really strange ideas and began straying from the basic proposition. All of a sudden, it wasn't about cheap, fast, tasty food anymore. McDonald's tried to be the one thing they're very definitely not — healthy. They bombed out with all kinds of fresh products, which the consuming public overwhelmingly spat out in disgust time after time.

They even went so far as to try to get people from the neighborhood to get up on their little McDonald's stages and entertain diners. This from a fast food joint that prided themselves on getting you *out* of there as fast as possible.

Big Time Solution: McDonald's should fire everyone in their research division and go back to doing what it does best. They should work from their strength, which is cheap, fast and tasty. They could extend that proposition, for example, by making the food even faster: why not institute delivery as part of the plan? Let's face it, the pace of life is getting faster, not slower. We all have to cut corners some place, and walking down the street or driving through the arches just takes too much time. If my restaurant made it fast and tasty, I'd do everything I could to make it fast and even more convenient.

6 **drkoop.com:** Someone tell me what went wrong with this one. Please. Here you have arguably the most personable Federal employee since Abraham Lincoln — despite the funny beard — and the best they were able to do with his warmth and humanity was not to feature it at all.

Have you been to this site yet? It's everything that Dr. Koop *isn't*: blatant ads thrown at your face. Sales pitches that make your traveling carnival pitchman look legitimate. In fact, they've thrown everything on to this website except what they should have: the old doctor himself. Instead, they offer up a weak excuse of a tagline, "Your trusted health network."

Clearly, the developers of this site totally forgot that trust is not a technological issue. It's a human issue. It's even more human when you consider that we're talking about stuff that people put in, on and around their own bodies.

Big Time Solution: Bring back the guy with the beard. The strength of the brand here isn't the message, but the messenger who delivers it. Instead of cold blacks, blues and whites, the venerable doctor should be surrounded by warm, comforting colors that stress his personal brand of reliability. The co-opters of this brand have a natural figurehead with tremendous leadership value. They should make him the brand icon.

7 **Timex:** Oh how the mighty have fallen. There was a time when you could ask anyone in America — maybe even the world — which wristwatch was the most durable, quality timepiece. Without hesitation, the answer would be, "Timex." Anyone who was breathing at that time can still remember the campy demonstrations Timex splattered all over the media, in which Timex watches "took a licking and kept on ticking."

Corny.

But effective.

Whatever franchise Timex enjoyed as the roughest, toughest timepieces evaporated long ago, however, the sickly victim of fashion-oriented watches like Swatch and famous name designers. Go to *http://www.timex.com* to see for yourself. There's no reason to buy one anymore. **Big Time Solution:** Who says you can never go home again? All the folks at Timex need to do is to take a look around to see that nobody has moved into their traditional niche. While Timex no longer owns the "affordable" category, their legacy is still strong. They could take back the durability niche in a heartbeat.

Their brand has taken a licking, but it still is ticking. The last I saw of Timex, they were capitalizing on their heritage with retro-based campaigns. It was a promising start.

8 **Metro-Goldwyn-Mayer:** Perhaps it's a testament to the rise of mediocrity in America, but there was a time when the crown jewel of Hollywood was MGM. For a good part of the last century, you knew you were in for a special kind of movie experience when it opened with Leo the lion announcing the first scene with his magnificent roar. There was a high class magnificence of the MGM brand that separated it from all other pretenders to the Hollywood throne.

No more.

While it is true that the entire film industry has pretty much melted down into one nepotistic compost heap, none of the studios ever matched the grandeur enjoyed by MGM. MGM *was* Hollywood. Today, however, it's just one more shell of a once-great brand, wholly vulnerable to any other dream merchant who has a father in the business.

Big Time Solution: MGM should follow the course that Miramax Studios blazed so skillfully in the 1980's, where niche audiences would attend the movies theater simply because the film was brought to them by Miramax. Whether they are known for family entertainment, adventure or just plain quality product, MGM needs to build on its heritage, not deplete it. In an industry that thrives on mimicking what the last guy did, MGM could take back its lead.

9 MCIWorldcom: It's only natural that companies evolve as they grow. And if there's anything you can say about MCI, it's that they've grown — really big. But somewhere along the way, MCI's discipline as a well-branded company got lost. When they started out, MCI was synonymous with "the low cost alternative to AT&T." I have no recollection as to what their tagline was, but through clever, impactful advertising, they made it extremely clear that telephone deregulation was here to stay, and that MCI was here to rescue America from high long distance rates.

Okay, so times have changed and MCI is obviously much, much more than a low rate long distance company. I have no issue with that. What I want to know is why I should choose MCIWorldcom today. The company used to excel at promoting its early virtues, but these days, its message is lost in a huge morass or undecipherable claims.

. Do you know why you should choose MCIWorldcom over anyone else? Neither do I.

Big Time Solution: MCIWorldcom needs to find something to hang its hat on and stick with it. Telecom's most critical issue is reliability, but AT&T holds that title. Sprint owned clarity of signal. What's left for MCIWorldcom? What about its ability to tailor programs to its most profitable user base — the business community? Of course, residential accounts are a piece of the puzzle, but nobody has yet claimed the title of the most responsive telecom company, nor the most professional. With its worldwide networks, MCIWorldcom could grab both.

10 **Seven-Up:** Someone once said that if you remember the sixties, you really weren't part of it — and they weren't talking about not being born yet. While many still struggle to recall those memories through a vast, drug-laden haze, the truth is that the sixties was a decade of creativity that spawned some of the most powerful media impressions in history. One reason for that is because there were few media outlets that almost everyone watched, so whatever you put out there was seen and integrated by an entire population overnight.

Another reason was the drugs
.   The media also helped spread the phenomenon and acceptance of the drug culture, which was a message of rebellion, creativity and spirituality all rolled into one. For the first time in history, going against the grain was a good thing. In fact, the more flamboyant you were about it, the more the public adored you for it.

And it was just as true for soft drinks as it was for the Beatles.

It was in that environment that Seven-Up drove its stake into the ground with a brand that remains its most memorable since that decade. By positioning itself as "the Un-Cola", Seven-Up rocketed in popularity with those who no longer wished to be perceived as part of the dominant "cola establishment." Seven-Up was — and still is, from what I hear — a clear soda, using lemon and lime juices as its main flavoring ingredients. It looked different. It tasted different. And in the 1960's, actually became a political statement.

Today, the colas are as prevalent as ever. But where is Seven-Up? Dangerously circling the drain is where. Somewhere along the line, the very same sensitivity that put them in touch with an entire generation's cultural values just evaporated. In their case, Seven-Up lost their courage to lead by example and settled into the "me-too" race with all the other "non-cola" beverages. Today, the Seven-Up brand stands for nothing at all, its former rebel status having been swiped from under its nose by Mountain Dew, a drink which succeeds despite its uncanny resemblance to carbonated urine.

Big Time Solution: The most tempting solution here would be to reach back to those drug-addled hippies and beg them to come back. But as John Lennon so aptly put it, "the dream is over." There is no going back to a generation whose tastes long ago shifted from "free love at Woodstock" to "free samples at K-Mart."

But the ever-youthful soda could identify itself with a psychographic by realizing that the rebel spirit never dies. By leveraging itself against its competitors' huge growth, Seven-Up could realize that the Mountain Dews of the market have grown to such size as to no longer represent credible rebels.

Seven-Up should become the underground beverage of choice, enjoyed and promoted by an online army who are smarter than the extreme bikers and Zog-toting surfers. The media implosion allows Seven-Up to pursue drinkers on a psychographic level, which means part of their cool is being enjoyed by grandma's and teens alike who share the same spirit, but not the same television viewing habits.

Of course I could write tons more, but my publisher won't let me. The point is that once you create a great brand, you've got to keep nurturing it or it will eventually die. That doesn't mean sacrificing your brand equity for every fashion or fad that comes along. But it does mean that your brand's core values have to be able to respond consistently to changing market conditions and still remain intact.

That's yet another hallmark of a Big Time Brand.

ACTION ITEMS — CHAPTER TWELVE

1. Choose a brand you used to worship

2. Think about why you loved it.

3. Analyze why you no longer love it.

4. Figure which brand took its place.

5. What could your original brand have done to prevent its demise?

13

WHEN GOOD BRANDS DO GOOD: 10 BRANDS THAT REALLY SING

I hate people who whine. And that includes myself. So I'm not going to crank out page after page telling you everything that's wrong and why everything sucks. The fact is that — although I didn't create them — there are some pretty darn good brands out there.

I mean really good.

The kind of brand that make you wish you had thought of them. The kind of brands you look at wistfully as they waltz down the street hand in hand with millions of end-users hanging on their every word, dying to fork over their hard-earned money. Big Time Brands go way beyond the call of duty in the marketplace. In fact, one of the hallmarks of a Big Time Brand is its ability to integrate itself into the parlance and cultures of society at large. People not only adopt these brands, but actually wrap themselves up in them, identifying and labeling themselves under that brand. That's why *trekkies* recognize each other at *Star Trek* conventions and members of my *FrankelBiz* list refer to themselves as *FrankelBees*.

So just in case you thought there weren't any, here are ten brands that I think really sing:

1 **Harley-Davidson:** There are some brands that have cultivated their allegiances so smartly as to actually incite violence at the thought of besmirching their good name. Harley-Davidson is such a brand.

Whether Harley-Davidson actually makes a better motorcycle is a subjective matter, at best. The one thing you *can*
bank on, however, is that it wouldn't be too smart to waltz
into a bar and yell, "My Honda can kick any hawg's butt!"
Which in and of itself is something of an indication of the
brand's success: they actually have their own slang. If you
know anything at all about them, I don't have to tell you what
a "Fat Bob" is.

If a real Harley fan were to 'fess up, he'd tell you that
it's not so much the bike as it is the Harley experience. The
legend. The cult. Even that distinctive low-throated rumble
that the United States Patent Office has recognized as one of
only three sounds its department protects.

Other motorcycle companies have tried to imitate the
Harley look and feel. But the brand is so strong that those
imitations elicit more peals of laughter than peeling rubber.

2 Apple Computer: Like Harley-Davidson, Apple
Computer was getting badly beaten in the marketplace
at one time. And just like the Harley, it was Apple's
diehard, brand-loyal fans that eventually came to their
rescue.

In a conversation with Regis McKenna, one of the
major forces behind the creation of Apple, he imparted a
story in which he went so far as to advise that the company
think about turning its attentions to licensing the Apple logo,
slapping in on anything and everything that could generate a
fee. He was only half-kidding, of course, but it spoke to the
strength of Apple's brand value to its end-users.

Decades after its inception — never having owned
the market the way Microsoft has — Apple still commands
so much loyalty that lone users in Windows-based networks
still prefer to customize their LAN's to accommodate their
Mac's. Just try finding the reverse situation. Never gonna

happen.

Perhaps because of Microsoft, Apple has managed to capitalize on a rebel *esprit de corps* among its users. The edgy, creative David against the evil, slothful Goliath. When Microsoft conquers 90% of the market, you don't hear Windows users cheering. But when Apple claws back into double digits, their entire universe orders out for pizzas and party hats.

Apple doesn't have a user base. They've got a cheering section. The hallmark of a Big Time Brand.

3 Federal Express: I'm sorry, but if I go on any more about this company's excellence in branding, the Senate will likely launch a corruption and bribery investigation about it. Enough said.

4 Rolls Royce: I don't drive one. I don't want one. But if there ever was a brand that immediately communicated its qualities in one fell swoop, it has to be the Buick from Britain. Ask the man who drives one, and he'll tell you that the Rolls Royce is simply the finest automobile ever created. It's also one of the most expensive, which only goes to prove my point about branding:

The difference between one commodity's value and another is its brand.

The brand is so well-seeded that it's been fully integrated into our culture. Listen closely to the flight attendants when they bark out emergency procedures on your next flight. They never call your attention to the jet engines powering the aircraft if they're manufactured by General Electric. But boy, are they proud of their Rolls Royce powered rockets. You'll hear them brag about them as if they park them in their own garages at night.

Rolls Royce has — without nearly as much mass media advertising as most — managed to niche its way up to the top of our consciousness, to the point where anyone positioning themselves as the best in the business frequently refers to themselves as "the Rolls Royce of" whatever sector they happen to inhabit.

The truth of the matter is that very little drops faster than the resale value of a Rolls. Which may say something about the car. And even more about the brand.

5 Craftsman (Sears): In my entire life, I maybe bought five things from Sears. For that matter, I've probably only been in a Sears store about five times. But every time I was in there, I bought the same stuff: Craftsman Tools.

The thing I like most about Craftsman is that it stands out like an oasis in the desert. While just about everything else in Sears stores is, well, Sears stuff, their brand of tools rises above to the most professional levels. Ask anyone — especially anyone who doesn't know very much about tools — and they'll gladly tell you all about Craftsman. How professionals use them. And how you can return them if they ever break — no matter how long ago you bought them.

Even when Sears lost a huge lawsuit against an inventor who gave them a great idea for a whole new tool set, it was Sears who took the publicity hit. The Craftsman brand was barely scratched and kept dancing as if nothing even happened.

Truth be told, Craftsman makes good stuff. But is it any better than Makita or other competing brands? Hard to tell. But in terms of branding, the boys from Sears win this one hands down.

6 DieHard (Sears): Can you believe it? Out of the zillions of brands out there, I give two of the top slots to Sears. Not because they're American as apple pie. And not just to prove that I'm really a lot nicer than people think. No, you've got to give credit where it's due and despite any other woes they may have, Sears certainly knew what they were doing when they branded their automobile batteries.

I should probably state that I have absolutely no idea as to whether the DieHard battery is the nation's leading battery. But it doesn't really matter. What does matter is that the DieHard battery is just about the only battery that even has a brand image. If you doubt that, drop this book right now and go ask your secretary or office assistant to name three car batteries. Ten to one says that he or she will not only be able to list this one brand, but also tell you its brand attributes.

True, the DieHard has enjoyed high awareness since the 1960's, when television commercials wove visions of snowbound cars turning over effortlessly with the twitch of an ignition key. But that's beside the point. The Sears team honed in on the one aspect of car batteries that hit home the hardest — their failure at inopportune and dangerous moments.

They even *named* it right.

Think it's no big deal? Think about this: How many car batteries can you name? And if that still doesn't impress you, consider the highly competitive world of household and toy batteries. Now, which one uses the bunny?

Are you *sure*?

7 **Southwest Airlines:** You want to talk about a commodity category, you don't have to go much further than the airline industry. And when it comes to competitive sectors, there's none moreso than the commuter corridors. Short-hop airlines take the most heat, cramming down fares on trips of a couple of hundred miles, marketed mainly to passengers who traditionally buy on price alone. The theory is that most of these passengers are business travelers who grin and bear whatever they have to while their bodies are shipped to the next meeting.

What a relief, then, to find a brand like Southwest that does whatever it can to make the process that much more enjoyable and convenient. If Southwest wasn't the first to offer free companion fares, they certainly shouted it the loudest. They did the same with no-reserved seating and faster boarding. They were among the first to embrace tick-etless travel, too. But all of those features pale in comparison to the infectious enthusiasm emanating from every employee.

And talk about extending the brand personality beyond the immediate marketplace: even their stock ticker is LUV.

8 Playboy: A rabbit. One stinkin' rabbit. Not even a *full-color* rabbit. Hardly illustrated beyond the detail of an international traffic sign and likely the most readily identifiable brand in the world of publishing. Hugh Hefner's branding of *Playboy* magazine was definitely no fluke. If there's anyone who was able to link vision with strategy, our pajama man has to be the one
.   To really understand the strategic vision of *Playboy*, you have to appreciate the fact that Hefner launched his empire well before there was even a hint of a sexual revo-lution. In that era, sex was something you did to have children — or so America hoped. Hef knew better than that. But he also knew that the last thing America needed was another under-the-counter nudie magazine.

Which is why *Playboy* is not about sex. It's about *class*. More evidence that Big Time Branding is less about what you sell than how you sell it.

At the time *Playboy* was launched, there were plenty of girlie magazines around. But there weren't any classy publications for men. *Playboy* cleverly mixed sex with music and fashion. It took *Gentlemen's Quarterly* and super-charged it with a dose of hard-edged reality. As the brand grew, so did its competition. In time, *Penthouse* even overtook *Playboy* in circulation numbers

But they never took *Playboy's* place as the *class entry* in men's brands.

Today, you don't see that many brands knocking on the doors of *Penthouse* or *Hustler* or any other internationally printed men's magazine. Not the way they clamor after *Playboy*. The brand reaches beyond its pages to sponsor music, fashion and just about everything else that wants to position itself as the classic men's product.

Despite the one-color rabbit.

9 Head & Shoulders Shampoo: Yes, it's old. Yes, it's boring. And, yeah, it probably is one of the most heavily-advertised hair care products out there. But the beauty of Head & Shoulders shampoo is that it has one clearly articulated purpose in life: to help you get rid of your dandruff.

The name is no great shakes. It's like naming a foot powder Heel & Toe. Yet despite the lack of creativity, generations of people with dandruff problems do indeed reach for Head & Shoulders first. More importantly, people who *don't* have dandruff problem know which brand to reach for if they ever do find their sweater littered with skin bits.

There are plenty of dandruff shampoos out there. And hair care products usually enjoy a shelf life of two to three years before they become yesterday's news. Not Head & Shoulders. This is one brand that never flakes out.

10 Disney: Personally, I can't stand the brand, but that doesn't mean that the rat with the pixie dust hasn't done an excellent job at branding himself and his merchandise. Ask any retailer in the country and you'll find that Disney manages to twist their arms for better terms and higher rates because they know that merchandise moves faster when a Disney tag is sewn on.

It's easy to pooh-pooh Disney in hindsight. But if you extend that hindsight a tad further, you'll find that not all that long ago, Disney was little more than an animation studio and a theme park. The world has seen lots of cartoons and thrill rides since, but few have equaled or surpassed Disney's success or longevity.

Although the bloom on their rose has wilted of late, realtors still gush like schoolgirls when hear a Disney store has leased out a space in their mall. Discerning five year old kids still choose Donald and Mickey over ninjas, rangers, tubbies or anything else when it comes to pajamas. And Disneyworld has to be the only place on the planet where people can be forced to pay over four dollars for one lousy hot dog.

But they do. Because they're willing prisoners in an environment that's strongly branded with the values and attributes they want.

The "happiest place on earth" has plenty of reason to be when it comes to brand strength. Disney's only danger now is over-saturating the market with its presence instead of relaxing and supporting it where necessary. Failing to do so will produce a customer backlash that won't be pretty.

11 Bonus Entry: The Apple Pan

I want to include one more brand that I think is doing a fabulous job, even though about 99% of you reading right now have no idea of who I'm talking about.

In west Los Angeles, there's a small hamburger stand that's been around since the Civil War. At least that's how old it seems to be. The Apple Pan sits at the corner of two busy streets. It's closed on Mondays. It has very limited seating around a horseshoe bar — and a line of people waiting to sit down at it.

The Apple Pan has weathered the invasion of McDonald's and Burger King. It has sat contentedly watching malls go up and coffee shops fall down.

Throughout it all, it continues to do what it does best: serve a quality hamburger and some of the best homemade pies you ever slid down your gullet.

People drive for miles just to have lunch there, which means The Apple Pan's branding strategy has paid off big time. Not through paid advertising (they don't do any). Not through stupid public relations ploys (they don't need any). Instead, they have managed to cater to the crowd that doesn't want McDonald's, or malls or anything else that comes with all the marketing trappings.

All they want is a decent hamburger, some pie and a cup of coffee. A place where they don't have to concern themselves with cholesterol counts and fat content. A place where you can just eat and not make such a big deal out of it.

I doubt that The Apple Pan ever employed a branding consultant. But if they did, he or she deserves a medal, if for nothing other than proving you can be a Big Time Brand without ever spending a cent.

ACTION ITEMS — CHAPTER THIRTEEN

1. Choose a brand that you wish you had branded.

2. Think about why you admire that brand so much.

3. How does that brand address its competition?

4. What about that brand can you emulate — okay, *steal* — and apply to your own company?

14

DOMAINIA

There are some aspects of the offline world that directly port to the online world. The bad news is that all too often, it's the bad habits that make the trip, not the good ones. In the offline world, people tend to make the mistake of thinking that a brand is little more than a logo, which we know by now is hardly the case. In the online world, people make the same mistake by thinking their domain name is all the branding they need.

Wrong-o-ritos.

To assume that a domain, or URL, is anything more than a piece of the brand structure is to go all the way back to page one of this book. A domain name is simply that: a name. An address on the world wide web that uniquely describes where people can find you. What most people don't realize is that URL's (Unique Resource Locators) actually exist on the web as numeric codes. They're usually a string of seven or eight or nine numbers — I forget how many, exactly — that are separated by three dots. Because numbers have an infinite supply of combinations, you can be assured that your site has its own unique combination of them. That combination is your Unique Resource Locator, or as the netteratti say, "URL."

Being the memory-challenged species we are, we mask the numeric URL's with alphanumeric names which are also not only guaranteed to be unique, but the subject of lawsuits, as well. That's because nobody was born with the name 206.124.224.2, but lots of folks were christened John

Smith. The result is that domains begin to take on different values.

There's no question that a domain name can add value to your web branding effort. In fact, there are at least three ways that domains can further your quest:

1 **Generic Value:** Let's face it, if you're in the bottling business, it probably can't hurt you to own *bottle.com* or *bottling.com* or *bottles.com* or just about every other variation of something that contains the word bottle. There's a certain wisdom that says *not* owning bottle.com is just plain foolish. It's your category. It's descriptive. And if you don't buy it, one of your competitors will.

I could even make the argument that as more people get familiar with the web, the more often they simply type in a "best guess" URL in their browser and hope that something they're looking for comes up. You can't blame them, either, because more often than not, what they're looking for usually does come up. And if it isn't exactly what they're looking for, it usually has clues as to where to search next. Of course, that doesn't always work, like if you type in brain-cancer.com, but let's not go there.

The point is that as people's patience dwindles even further, they're going to do everything they can to shorten their search for answers of the web. And as long as they type in something reasonably close to what they're searching for, a generic URL will get them close.

But don't kid yourself. While a generic URL might get you category hunters, it won't do anything for you in terms of branding. In fact, generic URL's actually work against your branding effort, because they're exactly that — generic. If your brand has any value at all, it goes against the grain of an established category. Which is why I consider generic domains to be highly overvalued. Of course, that didn't stop the owners of *beef.com* from offering up that URL for two million bucks, or *business.com* going for seven million. But is it really worth it? I mean, if I were Mickey's Meat Company, why would I want beef.com? The URL I want is MickeysMeat.com — because that's my brand.

Like I said, if there's a value to a generic URL, it's insurance. But be warned: even the best insurance isn't always worth the premium.

2 **Descriptive Value:** One step removed from the Generic URL is the Descriptive URL Descriptive URL's kind of dance around the brand concept they're trying to identify. Sites like *JustBalls.com* pretty much say what they are: nothing here that isn't round or doesn't bounce. And like their generic cousins, Descriptive URL's have a slight leg up on other URL's because they mention their category in their name. This can come in handy with search engines that count URL descriptions in the site rankings.

But just because a site tells you what it does doesn't mean it tells you why it's a better solution. And that's where descriptive URL's fall short. Don't get me wrong, here. I'm not saying that a Descriptive URL isn't a good way to go. I'm saying it's far from the best way to go.

And I think you're worth the best — don't you?

3 **Branded Value:** Last stop for this train. I like branded URL's because they say who they are and why you'd be nuts to look anywhere else. The other thing I like about branded URL's is that because they're uniquely designed to communicate your specific brand qualities, by definition nobody else can lay claim to them.

And when nobody else can claim them, that means you're the only one in the boat left to choose. You're branded. People who are loyal to brands are loyal to branded URL's, not generic or descriptive domains. And those are the domains that sell for big bucks when your exit strategy kicks in.

The Value of Domains

Your URL has a far greater impact on your web's brand than may reveal at first. A well-branded URL sits in a nice little corner of your company's balance sheet. It is by all means a tangible asset. An instrument of goodwill that commands a premium price.

Which means that URL's can come into play as a means of revenue, as well. And though I consider it to be a form of branding suicide, it's probably worth side-tracking a bit here to talk about buying and selling URL's.

For those who are new to the web, weirdest part of domainia is the "for sale frenzy" that can take on characteristics of the greater Internet IPO phenomenon. All of a sudden, somebody gets an idea that a domain like *beef.com* is really worth two million. Or that *altavista.com* was worth three. The fact is that when Compaq paid three million for *altavista.com*, they weren't paying for the domain's value — they were paying a nuisance fee that their lawyers couldn't win.

When Panavision sued to get their *panavision.com* domain back, however, they got it in a heartbeat because the judge felt the original owner was holding the company up for ransom. Despite his protestations — and they were pretty imaginative — the original owner of *panavision.com* was forced to surrender the URL for cost.

No matter how ridiculous people's valuations for their domains are, even more people jump on the bandwagon with completely silly URL's demanding even more. Clearly, someone needs to set down some thinking here. Might as well be me.

Look, I'm as greedy as the next guy, but let's temper our enthusiasm with a little thinking, shall we? Just because white men in blue suits buy Amazon stock at $100 or $200 a pop doesn't mean the stuff is worth it. By now, you should realize that valuations are usually driven by frenzy — the real work is done by CPA's who try to convince the public that those share prices actually have some basis in reality.

Right.

But if you really do plan on selling your domain, let me offer you one piece of advice that could save you big bucks: don't offer it for sale. The rules have changed in these past few years. It used to be that domains went on a "first come, first served" basis. Not any more. Sure, you can register a domain with Internic or any one of a dozen services, but these days, domains are considered extensions of intellectual property, like patents and copyrights. Which means that even if you registered *cocacola.com* back in 1992, you ain't gonna keep it, pal. The lawyers won't let you and the courts will back them up.

So how do you squeeze a few bucks in the name of free trade?

Well, one way is by approaching an interested party and suggesting a joint venture possibility. But the true bull's eye strategy is *not* to promote a domain for sale. You're far better off to buy one you think will fetch big bucks. Then, when people start sniffing around, asking you what you're doing with the domain, you simply answer thusly:

"Ummm, the site's in planning stages right now, but what did you have in mind?"

If you answer like that, the caller has to figure that you have a real stake in the name and won't sic his lawyer on you. This happens a lot when people have personal names that coincide with those of giant corporations. My friend Jaclyn Easton owns Easton.com — how happy do you think the folks at Easton baseball bats were about that? But it's her name, and there's nothing they could legally do about it.

I happen to own *buyatcost.com*, which is a nice generic phrase and because it is so generic, I feel confident that nobody will ever try to pry it away from me, unless their name happens to be something like Melvin H. Buyatcost. I also own *metroliner.com*, which I suppose Amtrak could try to monkey with, if it weren't for the fact that I purchased it for a client with that name.

Of course, if you're interested, those sites are in planning stages right now, but what did you have in mind?

Alternative URL's: The Best Marketing Strategy

So what's the best strategy for selecting a URL? Which one is the best for you? The answer, surprisingly, is all of the above. Because what most people don't realize is that you can have as many alternative URL's point to the your site as you want. URL's are not sold on a one name, one site basis.

Generic and ancillary URL's are great for catching that traffic that doesn't know you by your brand name yet. And there's nothing in the rules that says people absolutely MUST find you by your brand name. So you might as well play the odds. After all, it costs you what — maybe $35 per URL per year to pick up those strays? What a deal!

I recommend alternative — or generic if they're lucky enough — URL's for clients, as long as they don't invest a dime in promoting them. Put your money behind the _branded_ URL, let the others be the icing on the cake.

That's why _robfrankel.com_ will get you to my site — but so will _brandingexpert.com, bigtimebranding.com, brandingconsultant.com, brandedcomunity.com, brandedcommunities.com, brandedcommunity.com, marketconsulting.net and marketconsulting.com._

Yes, folks. It's the very same obnoxious bobbing head.

Of course, I put all the money behind _robfrankel.com_, because that's where the brand is. But that doesn't mean those other little helpers can't drag in a wild lead or two.

And as long as Internic keeps selling them at the bargain rate, it's a buyer's market.

ACTION ITEMS — CHAPTER FOURTEEN

1. Think of as many domain names (URL's) for your company as you can

2. Which is the most generic?

3. Which one most describes or proejcts your brand most accurately?

4. How many can you come up with that *don't* include your company's name?

5. Which URL captures and conveys your prospects' solutions?

15

BRANDING AND TECHNOLOGY

As the web has evolves from geek to greed, there's an issue with which everyone eventually has to grapple. Call it the Eternal Struggle. The Battle of the Binaries. But sooner or later, you're going to have to deal with the issue of just how much technology serves to strengthen your brand on the web.

Or kill it off entirely.

See, a lot of newbie types make the egregious error of assuming that the geekier the site, the more legitimate it looks. Nothing could be further from the truth.

The camps pretty much fall along the lines you'd expect if you announced you were taking the company on a trip to Las Vegas: the marketing guys think they're going to a money-driven funfest while the techno-geeks start packing their bags figuring they're going to spend the week trading new codes on the floor of a COMDEX show.

Sure, technology plays a big part of web strategy. But it has nothing to do with creating and maintaining a strong, viable brand. In fact, if you're not careful, the same technology that allows you to beat the phone company out of a long distance telephone charge can shipwreck all of your marketing and branding efforts. The mantra to keep chanting is that *technology doesn't drive branding, people drive branding*. Technology drives people nuts.

And don't listen to anyone who rants about how other technologies have been marketed, because you're not in the business of marketing technology. You're in the business of marketing whatever it is you're marketing.

So how do you know when enough technology is enough? Well, let's take a little drive down that road and discuss what works – and what doesn't.

The Cutting Edge is for Schmucks.

It happens to everyone. Another year gone by and even more of your online and offline computer technology has become outdated. Not obsolete. Just a little old. A little dusty.

This is the time of year when you take a look around your somewhat disheveled office, pick through the paper clips and take stock of exactly how far you've fallen behind the rest of the techno-world. Glancing around the office, you see not-so-recent versions of Microsoft This or Claris That. Shrink-wrapped boxes and manuals of version 8 point something that you swore you'd read some time last summer.

Face it. You're old. You're out of it. You are no longer cutting edge.

But that's okay. You know why? You REALLY want to know why? Okay, huddle closer and I'll tell you:

The cutting edge is for schmucks.

That's right. You read correctly. The cutting edge is for schmucks. Dopes. People who don't know any better. Now if you think I'm just rattling this stuff off the top of my head, well, you're partially right. But I'm also right for a number of reasons, which I shall now enumerate:

First, people who insist on being cutting edge basically have nothing to offer other than being the first at something. Big deal. Unless you actually own something outright, there's absolutely no point in being first at it. Think about it. You can invent the first online technology that streams a hot cheese pizza to end users complete with anchovies and lossless compression and if there isn't anyone on the receiving end with that technology, who cares? It's useless!

The problem is bad enough with all the useless software upgrades being foisted on you and me, but it really gets ugly when you start cruising the internet to visit these "cutting edge" sites.

I don't know about you, but I consider myself a pretty sophisticated net guy. But just try logging on to the net's latest sweetheart site with "cutting edge" technology and my little browser goes into all kinds of fits and conniptions and finally freezes because it's been blindsided — yet again — by some sort of weird "cutting edge" technology that hasn't even been given a name yet.

One guy uses Java applets, another uses Shockwave. And neither one of them offers a NON-Java or NON-Shockwave version of their site for me to browse! I can't get into their sites even if I wanted to.

Cutting Edge? That's fine for guys like Gates and Jobs and folks whose business is dazzling Wall Street with visions of cyber gold. But for everyday guys like you and me, I can tell you that cutting edge technology sucks. The minute you adopt it, somebody either has a newer version or a different platform, neither of which really matters to you, because both are totally incompatible with whatever you have running on your – or your prospective customer's — machine.

Okay, so if Cutting Edge isn't happening, what is?

The answer, my friends, is where you'd least expect it. The place where all your friends back in high school laughed at you. Where all your co-workers snicker at you and wherever *People* magazine isn't spotlighting some larger than life personality that's bound to be parking cars this time next year:

Yes, the really cool place to be is: *behind the times.*

That's right. Being where it's at isn't what you want; being where it's *been* is where it's at.

Hmmm. Let me explain that.

By staying at least two cycles behind the cutting edge

of technology, you're assured that people with slower machines and antique browsing capability can access your website. And believe me. There's more of them than there are of us. Why? Well consider this: even the lowliest of Windows lovers will concede that less than half of all PC users have loaded Windows ninety-something on to their machines. And despite what you read in this week's computer superstores' newspaper ad, most users out there are still running on something that hasn't seen the light of a computer retailer's store for at least three years.

Not exactly cutting edge in the hardware department, if you get my drift.

And modem speed? Sure, *you* might have a 56K flex. You might even be humming along on an ADSL line or a satellite dish, thumbing your nose at the rest of the 28.8's who wait half an hour to download a twenty second video clip of people doing things to each other that were once considered physically and structurally impossible.

No, my friend, when it comes to the web, *accessibility* is what makes it happen. Which means the less accessible you are, the less chance that anyone who comes knocking at your door will ever end up buying. Conversely, the further away you are from the cutting edge, the more accessible your website becomes to all us cyber have-nots, bringing you troves of wealth to lay at your feet.

If you want a little glamour, okay, throw in an animated GIF here and maybe a stable javascript there. There's your glamour. Otherwise, leave the cutting edge stuff to the big boys. They're the ones who can afford to throw a party and have nobody show up.

Call me old fashioned. Call me a wet blanket. Lose the cutting edge stuff, and you can definitely call me profitable.

Five kinds of techno-junk that can kill your website

If you're beginning to get the idea that there are a lot of technological ways to screw up your web site, you're dead on the money. I suppose I make such a big deal about it because to most people, the web strikes them as a technologically-driven medium, when in reality, it's a human-driven medium that's no more dependent on technology than television, radio or print. So it makes no sense to attempt to derive marketing solutions from technological means. After all, you don't get more efficient newspaper advertising by printing on different kinds of paper.

The point here is to make your technology as transparent as possible so that your brand comes shining through. In that spirit, here are my five favorite ways that technological knowledge – or lack thereof – can really derail your website:

1 **Wide Screens are for movies**. Many businesses make their first mistakes at the very start of a website project, by hiring designers instead of marketing people. The problem with designers is that most of them work with 20 inch monitor screens, which means they have absolutely no problem viewing a 1,028 pixel wide home page in millions of colors. For the record, the zillions of people on the internet are using screens that can barely hold an image measuring 640 pixels across, and most of them can read only 256 colors.

So forget the wide-screen thing. Limit your designer to a working space of no more than 600 — that's right, you've got to allow about 40 pixels for browser junk — pixels across. It'll save your viewers tons of scrolling, clicking and screen refreshing time.

2 <blink>**BLINKING IS ANNOYING**</blink>. Okay, so you finally learned a few cute HTML tricks, among which are little style tags that make your copy blink. If

you look up "annoying' in the dictionary, you're likely to
find it there. Contrary to popular notions that blinking copy
attracts viewer attention, the truth is that blinking copy
actually distracts viewers from the real purpose of the page.

One more reason to trash your blinking tags is that it
has a nasty habit of taking extra characters out of the line-
up: often, the few letters following a blink tag disappear
entirely.

3 **Uncork those plug-ins.** Hey, you ever been down
THIS road before? You log on to a really cool web site
that purports to have really neat stuff. "Click Here!" it
tells you, noting that you're just one touch away from the
greatest thing since Cindy Crawford's workout video. You
click the mouse and — a notice pops up telling you where
to go to find the plug in you're going to need to view the
greatest thing since Cindy Crawford's workout video.

Right. I'm going to log off the site, download the
plug-in, re-boot the browser, log back on to the site after
installing the plug? Man, who has time for that? Better I
should click over to your competition who won't waste my
time.

The point here is that until various plug-ins are
common-place among the vast majority of users – or better
yet, non-existent — I don't go near them and neither should
you. Sure, there are some great gimmick technologies out
there, but it doesn't mean you need to use them. Especially
if they're costing you business.

If you absolutely must destroy someone's dial-up
connection, at least do it with a technology that's included
with the browser at installation. Then pray that those users
didn't turn the plug in off.

4 **Ban those banners.** There I said it. I know, this is
going to get me in trouble with almost everyone I
know, but let me just explain before you whack out

your hate mail. Banners are fine for the folks who are equipped to handle them properly. But those people are few and far between for a couple of reasons.

First, for banner ads to work, you've got to attract mega-volumes of viewers. If you don't draw them, whose going to pay for a banner on your site? Second, to really manage your banner program well, you've got to rotate and target them all over your ever changing content. If that's not your thing, the most you'll ever make off of banner revenue will just cover your next tab at Starbuck's. If you're serious about generating revenue, the time has come for you to get serious about developing a specialty niche and concentrating on a brand-compatible sponsors for that niche. Get someone to plunk down bucks on a site where they have an interest of a viewer and the credibility of a long term partner.

Again, just because ad banner technology is available doesn't mean it's right for you.

5 Enough with the streaming copy. I don't know about you, but I view lots of weird pages that download in the freakiest ways. Most of the time I have to watch the document load and wait until I see a message that says, "Document Done" before I know the document has actually finished loading. So the last thing I want is an annoying little line of moving type that pitches me information that's already up there on the home page: "For a great pencil eraser, call Erasers-R-Us at 1-800-000-0000! Ask about our Ink Eraser 2 for 1 special!"

Terrific. Exactly how much closer to the sale will a message like that move me, when it really only serves to piss me off? Nine times out of ten, if I guess when the page has finished loading, I'm wrong and I have to re-load the page...while grumbling.

So why do I write about the stuff that doesn't work? Well, the way I figure it, there are thousands of public relations people smiling and dialing their way around the media, trying to convince everyone that their technologies and media are the Next Big Thing. But the fact is that very few of these NBT's ever work right out of the gate — or even way on down the road. So it's left to guys like me to tell you what's out there and why you shouldn't buy into it. At least not yet.

After all , you're trying to build your business, not theirs. Before you access any new technology or strategy. make sure it's something that's in your interest — not just in fashion.

Does that mean that you should junk any new-fangled technology that happens to download your way? Nah. But it does mean that you should be careful. It might even mean that there's some technology that you need to add to your site.

A few, in particular, come to mind.

ACTION ITEMS – CHAPTER FIFTEEN

1. List three technologies – online – that will further your brand the most.

2. List three technologies – offline – that will further your brand the most.

3. Which technologies are so incompatible with your brand that they would actually *undermine* your brand's value?

4. Find at least one totally worthless piece of technology in your company that everyone knows is worthless, but is too afraid to speak up about.

5. Find three technologies currently in operation in your company that could be tweaked to become branded to your company.

16

BRANDING TOOLS FOR THE WEB

Technology that works: Fulfillment & Response

To respond or not respond, that is the question. Actually, that's not the question, but it makes a pretty dramatic opening line. The real question I want to discuss is centered more on something web people don't talk about much:

What do you do with people who actually respond to your sales pitch?

Specifically, is it smarter to make them click through your site to order your product or service? Or should you feature a toll free phone number for them to call? As usual, there are plenty of answers, most of which revolve around the issue of what kind of business you're operating.

For now, let's restrict the discussion to sites that sell actual product or services.

I don't know about you, but I have a real hard time with businesses that go to all the trouble of building and publicizing a web site, only to have me call them on the phone to actually buy stuff. I mean, you've got me here, standing in your virtual showroom. Why wouldn't you simply sell me what you've got with a simple mouse click? It seems awfully silly to make me fumble around with the telephone, especially when I may only have one phone line to begin with. What am I supposed to do, sign off and call you back?

Man, that really frosts my cursor. The only things that freeze it harder are (1) tightwads that want ME to pay for the call to buy THEIR stuff and (2) web cadets that offer no way to contact them online to ask them questions before I purchase.

Ah, I feel better.

Okay, I hear a lot of keyboards tapping out replies already, saying "Hey, Rob — not everyone can afford to build secure servers with sophisticated order entry and delivery systems." To which I hastily reply, "Who says that NOT doing it is any cheaper?" The fact is that when you look at all the hidden and long term costs, NOT installing an automated system can cost you way more bucks than would chunking down a few bills now. Besides, almost everyone and their mother has a cheap, off-the-shelf e-commerce system that you can work from your browser. What's the big deal?

Remember that order-taking online is a 24 hour a day, 365 days a year option. A dynamic, secure server never calls in sick. Never complains about temporary water weight gain. And doesn't frustrate customers with answers like, "Gee, I don't know, they didn't tell us that — can you hold?"

Another consideration is the fact that no matter how cheap your flat rate is, toll-free numbers cost money. It doesn't matter why the caller calls, either. Every so often, my phone rings because the knucklehead who dialed it confused my toll-free "888" prefix with a toll-free "800" prefix, costing me time and money to explain over his objections that no, I am not a credit dentist and that his insurance co-payment is his problem, not mine.

Still another reason to think about secure servers is the fact that the only person who can screw up the order is your customer himself. A good click-dependent fulfillment structure not only takes the order, but send the customer a confirmation by e-mail, restating the order and terms. When was the last time your Customer Service Rep at Victoria's Secret did that for you?

Yet another benefit of automating your fulfillment operations is that you can instantly track your activity without having to rely on an assistant associate supervising manager to create the report for you. No lost data. No "garbage input". Just pure, virgin data.

Mmmmm, yummy.

Finally, my favorite reason for automating fulfillment: it makes you look big. Really big. In a world filled with ten speed bicycle web sites, automated fulfillment makes you look like a Cadillac. And not one of those wimpy little Credenzas or whatever they're calling those fuel-efficient latter day Caddies. I'm talking long, shiny black Fleetwood with dual exhausts and a TV antenna in the back. Think about your competition — do they offer that kind of service? Of course not. Why? Because they're afraid of the cost, even though almost every piece you need is off-the-shelf stuff.

Admit it: don't YOU feel better about a site when you see how slick their order-taking process is? Sure you do. Because it makes the site look and feel more established and credible.

That increases sell-through. It vaults your customer loyalty. And that's the kind of experience that shellacs your brand image directly to the frontal lobe of every customer who clicks on it.

What you're missing can hurt you, too.

Of course, now that we're talking about technology that really is useful, we might as well take a look at technology whose absence can really mess you up. Typically, those are the response technologies. Things like follow ups. And order confirmations. Most of the time, these are lumped together under the broad generic term "autoresponders." But that really doesn't do them justice. Because that's only the technological description. When it comes to building your brand, these little puppies can make you or break you.

Sure, fulfillment is sexy. But customers remember you —and your brand — for the stuff that happens *after* you've sucked the money out of their wallets. In the words of the old crooners, little things mean a lot. And in most cases, they provide opportunities for you to showcase how different your brand really is. The little things also take up an enormous amount of your valuable time. Fortunately, most of them can be automated on the web with autoresponders, the online equivalent of robots that write letters and perform repetitive tasks that would drive ordinary people like you and me insane.

One of the best uses of an autoresponder is a customer order verification. Nothing says "I love you" more than an e-mail to a customer that arrives immediately after their purchase, assuring them that their order has been accepted and confirmed with their very own tracking number. If you're really pro, you include a complete list of what business was transacted and when the customer can expect the next step in the process. If you're selling stuff, that means you describe what they bought and how soon they can expect to receive it.

Autoresponders are at their best when they confirm information. They're at their *worst* when abused the way morons concoct "personalized" mail-merged letters that are so blatantly un-personal that they actually alienate the very people they're supposed to endear. So avoid using autoresponders for e-mailing anything other than simple "thank you" and confirmation messages. Keep in mind that the way you've composed your auto-response message is a perfect vehicle for extending your brand. Simply chucking them a "thanks for the order, sucker" obviously doesn't leave your customers with the yearn to return. A message that compliments their wise choice, followed up with an assurance of how much you appreciate their business does much better.

And if you really are sharp, you include a discount code they can apply to their next purchase.

Chat rooms

I wanted to save this little creature for last, because it's really a super example of how technology alone is rarely a solution — and can actually cause more grief than it solves.

I'm going to save talking about chat rooms and other brand-building community tools for the next chapter, where you'll see exactly how far they can power your brand — or torpedo its credibility entirely.

ACTION ITEMS – CHAPTER SIXTEEN

1. Write the most personal autoresponse letter you can – that doesn't sound, look or feel like an autoresponder.

2. List all the occasions and opportunities in your business operations where autoresponses would be appropriate – and why.

3. List all the occasions where the use of autoresponses would be totally *inappropriate* and why

4. Create three totally new places where mundane and repetitive tasks ordinarily done by humans could be more effectively achieved and brand-strengthening through the pure use of technology.

5. Go through your company's web site and identify which technologies possess a true utilitarian or branding value and which are there because the designer thinks "they're cool".

17

THE BRANDED COMMUNITY

Some of the most talked-about subjects — at least among the advertising types on and offline — are how to drive traffic and increase response rates. Offline, the rule of thumb for response rates goes something like this: you can expect 1% to 3% response when you do a "random" direct mail campaign. By "random", I mean a campaign where you either buy a direct mail list or broadcast your message through some other medium. If you happen to be able to target you audience, you might expect those numbers to notch up a point or two, but not much more than that.

The common wisdom has always been, "if we just run enough eyeballs past it, one or two per cent are bound to fall into our bucket, even if it's by accident." And that works — to a point — if you have zillions to invest for a 1% return. Direct mail catalogs, for example, defoliate rain forests to the tune of millions of catalogs per years, breaking the backs of postal carriers everywhere on the off chance that one or two per cent of their recipients will pony up a few bucks and make the whole thing worth it.

That's a lot of money. A lot of *wasted* money, if you look at it from the other end: 97% to 99% of that money ends up on the floor. Down the tubes. Gone forever.

Raising response rates to 10% and 25%

One thing you can bet your last buck on is that anyone who finds 1% to 3% response rates acceptable for their business is probably not investing their own money in it. For everyone else, return on investment makes the difference between financial freedom and crawling back to that horrible corporate gig with your tail between your legs. And don't let those made-a-million-their-first-day-going-public stories fool you: it will be years, even decades before a lot of the Wall Street darlings ever make a dime profit. What will happen — a lot sooner than anyone thinks — is a lemming-like run to profitable companies, once those imaginative investors finally see a viable alternative.

The key to establishing higher response rates? You guessed it: a solid brand.

A well-constructed brand forms the basis of higher returns because the very nature of the brand is to be easily articulated by consumers. The more easily they can articulate your differentiating solution, the more readily they accept it — and evangelize it. That means more referrals, which in turn triggers greater growth.

Of course, a brand alone is only the foundation for that growth. The real opportunity for increasing response rates comes from the creation of a *branded community*.

Building a branded community

What, exactly, is a branded community? Unfortunately, most business keepers think it's just a bunch of customers dumped into a database, suitable for mailing tacky one-color postcards announcing inventory blowout sales.

Well, it's more than that. A lot more.

The keystone of a branded community is recognizing that its constituents — your customers — all have one thing in common: an affinity for your brand. That's all you can count on. And *that's* why building the right brand is so fundamentally important. You see, by creating the right brand, you create a personality. A fun-to-be-with entity with one or more distinguishing characteristics that people actually enjoy. The more they enjoy your brand, the more of the brand they *want* to enjoy.

They actually seek out opportunities to further their enjoyment of your brand, which translates into higher returns on just about anything you put in front of them — as long as it's an outgrowth that remains faithful to your brand. And that's how you start building your branded community.

How to build a branded community

The one thing that nobody else will tell you about building a solid brand is that by doing so, you not only increase customer loyalty, you also increase your profitability because you end up creating ancillary products, programs and services that ordinary competitors would never dream of. By building programs around your brand, you create an environment that supports your brand. And any environment that supports your brand — built properly — is going to reflect the same qualities that your loyal following adores so much. Which means the more you build, the more they enjoy.

And the more they enjoy, the better you do.

The E-Mail List: #1 Tool for Building Community

Once you begin building programs based on the community's common interest in your brand, the fun never stops, mainly because each module you bolt on improves, augments or extends the last. The more programs you build, the more involved your community members become. So much so, that if you play it right, you can actually expect them to begin suggesting programs of their own. And since I never prescribe a medicine I haven't experimented on myself, this seems as good as any place to illustrate my point.

For every site intent on building community, I strongly advocate establishing at least one *e-mail list*. An e-mail list is also called a *discussion list*, and is simply an e-mail-driven communications link between members. Each user subscribes to your e-mail list's e-mail address, authorizing them to post their messages to, and receive messages from, everyone else on the list. So if your list has a thousand people registered, you may post a message to the e-mail list server, which then broadcasts your message to all one thousand members via e-mail. Each member reads your message, and if they feel so inclined, they respond by posting their responses to the e-mail list server, which in turn, get broadcast out to the members, and so on. Within a relatively short amount of time, list members begin forming relationships around the issues that brought them together in the first place, and the foundation for your community is set.

E-mail list discussion lists are definitely the killer weapon in your community arsenal, for several reasons:

1 **E-mail lists are ridiculously inexpensive to create**. For less than $100 per month, you can rent software and space on a server that a third party maintains expressly for that purpose. You can even get e-mail list services for free, but if you do, be warned that the "cost" of those free e-mail lists is that every recipient is exposed to additional advertising with every message. For that reason, I strongly recommend you cough up the $100 per month and maintain total control of your content.

2 **E-mail lists are also very easy to maintain.** Most contemporary software allows you to control every aspect of list management through the web, using a standard web browser, like Netscape of Internet Explorer. By following easy menus, you point and click to customize and manage the list to the specifications you desire. You don't have to learn any software or hardware lessons.

3 **Because they're so easy to maintain, e-mail lists are also eminently customizable.** You can choose whether your members receive each message on its own, or grouped together into one day's worth of messages (digest mode). Customization includes nifty features like *headers* and *footers*, which automate the process of tagging every message with your pre-written message at either the top or the bottom of each message. Change it once, and the change takes effect immediately on every message each member receives.

Many sites make the mistake of using only one general e-mail list for their members. But in light of their low cost, smart brand managers keep watch on the threads of discussion and invariably "spin off" strong topics into their own dedicated lists. As the community grows, so does membership (often multiple memberships) of these lists. The community views this growth as responsiveness to their needs and wants.

As they always do, a minority of list members dominate the activity on the list, inviting interaction among others. You will find that this minority will do a lot of the marketing of the list for you, provided the list is well-managed. Many people use the list as an outlet for social interaction they otherwise would not have. If their experience is positive, many of them — and the "lurkers" who receive the messages but may not actively participate themselves — will evangelize the list to their peers. This brings their peers — themselves the most likely prospects for your brand — into your brand environment exactly the way you'd want them to be imported: through credible third party endorsements.

Since e-mail list messages are e-mail, almost all modern day e-mail reading applications automatically convert words beginning with "http" as hyperlinks that take the reader to that URL's site simply by clicking on the link. When the link is located on your site, it helps encourage visits on an impulse basis.

When you create a e-mail list, the ISP hosting the e-mail list will ask you to create an e-mail address to which all posts should be sent. I strongly recommend choosing an address that includes your brand name, like partners@YourBrand.com for say, a group involving singles or romance issues. Building brand awareness is a function of frequency, and nothing builds frequency like receiving e-mail from the same address several times a day. Responding to the list also requires a brand impression, as members address their responses to the same e-mail address.

4 **A critical component of branding is assuming the mantle of leadership**. In the matter of discussion lists, this falls to the FAQ's (Frequently Asked Questions) to shape and inspire the brand's vision of what the e-mail list is for, what is acceptable and what is not. I strongly recommend establishing an individual to take charge of *moderating* the list and enforcing the FAQ's. I make this recommendation for two reasons:

First, a visible leader provides an authority figure to whom the rest of the list looks for guidance, enforcement and sometimes, information. It is the Moderator's responsibility to approve or reject each message for posting. If the Moderator accepts the post, it goes out to the list. If the Moderator rejects the post, he should return the post to the sender with an explanation as to why it got booted. Which brings me to the second reason for recommending the installation of a Moderator.

The second reason I recommend a Moderator is that the Moderator is the personification of your brand. The comments he or she provides, and more importantly, *the manner in which those comments are put forth* should be viewed as extensions of the company's brand personality. How the brand conveys its personality comes through very clearly in this environment, subtly influencing the opinions of list members in a thoroughly *non-business* environment.

While most e-mail lists allow members to subscribe to the list via e-mail, I strongly recommend you not do so, but instead drive the member to your site where he or she can fill out a quick form which he or she can submit with a click. There are three compelling reasons for forcing members to sign up at your web site:

First, by eliminating sign ups by e-mail, you are displaying your intention to control the quality of the list member's experience. When you allow members to sign up by sending a message to the server by e-mail, the member has no exposure to your brand personality, ethics, values or culture.

Second, by driving the member to your website to enroll, you immediately expose them to your brand culture and mission. Lest we forget that the purpose of your site is to promote business, let's keep in mind that if people don't visit the site, they can't do business with it. So urging them to join the e-mail list at your site only makes sense. It exposes them to your business.

Third, by having members fill out a form, you can begin to form an idea about the kind of people to whom your brand is compelling. I usually ask for no more than four of five pieces of innocuous information: first name, e-mail address, business category and zip code. Make sure that the form specifies that all fields must be filled out properly, or the server will kick it back to them. Four fields of information is hardly intrusive, but you'll be amazed at how helpful they'll be when your list grows to hundreds or thousands of members. All kinds of trends and patterns begin to emerge, some of which you never would have suspected.

Always have a member confirmation device attached to the enrolling process, which may sound complicated, but only means the following: Make sure that the person who signed up for the list actually was the one signing up. There are pranksters out there who will sign up their enemies to hundreds of lists as a way of annoying them. The result is that you get hate mail and a reputation as a spamming entity, which is the online equivalent of the mark of Cain.

To avoid pranksters, I urge you to develop a member confirmation device, and the best one I know of is a member's confirmation of your FAQ's. Here's how it works:

After the member fills out the enrollment form at your site, he or she clicks on the "Submit" button, which sends the form to the server. The server receives the message and immediately sends the new member an e-mail containing your e-mail list's FAQ's, along with the instructions to "reply to this message to indicate your acceptance of these FAQ's and authorization to join the list." By doing so, you actually have completed two tasks: exposing the member to your guidelines and confirming their subscription. In both cases, you're sending the member another implicit message: *This is how we respect you and your privacy. It's part of how we do business.*

How e-mail lists evolve a brand: FrankelBiz case study

Back in the days when my main line of business was *Advertising, Marketing & Killer Creative*™, I began writing articles for an online advertising web site. Although I've never been one to shy away from expressing my opinions publicly, I now freely admit that the articles had less to with espousing curmudgeonly commentary on the advertising industry than it did with generating new business. Week after week, I would write my articles — I was Mr. Wednesday — and week after week, I would get a warm, loving call from the publisher, thanking me for writing a "great piece."

Then one day, I managed to find out *why* the publisher was calling so regularly. It seemed that over the few months I'd been writing, Mr. Wednesday was pulling in readers at a phenomenal rate — out-pulling other daily contributors by a impressive margin. When I put that together with the fan mail I was getting, it finally hit me:

There was a quality in my style that was building a brand loyalty. My audience, it seems, was interested in someone who cut through the crap and offered real solutions. They wanted honesty. And so what began as a free subscription of my articles soon grew into a community of like-minded individuals, bent on making the web a successful tool for their businesses. They had high ethics and low tolerances for the overblown, under-delivered promises that the "web professionals" were pushing at them. The community was clearly fed up with all the talk about commerce on the web.

So I named the community *FrankelBiz*. The web's first transaction list where we do business instead of whining about it. A major defining feature of the brand was its FAQ's, which each member had to approve before he or she could receive the service. By writing the FAQ's in a manner that was consistent with our rebellious spirit, members understood at the outset that this was no ordinary list. So the brand personality was able to deliver on each member's expectations.

The major branding distinction here was the fact that the list's FAQ's strictly *prohibited* discussion. The last thing anyone wanted in their e-mail was more discussion about last week's discussions. We were here to do business and help each other grow our businesses. It really worked.

And then it started happening.

The first community added value was free publicity. In what would be considered heresy on any other list, members began announcing their businesses to the other members, introducing themselves as solutions to other members' problems. Next, I fostered the notion that offering FrankelBiz discounts to FrankelBiz members was a show of good faith. Third, I offered up the concept that asking for help was just as important as offering a solution, which doubled the amount of opportunity placed in front of the community.

Yes, the name was self-serving. But I'm a businessman, not a nun. The branding of FrankelBiz was very specifically designed to incorporate my brand — the brand called Rob Frankel — right up there, where everyone could see it. The strategy was simple: the more successful the community became, the more readily I would be identified with it. And as a consultant, it not only made lots of sense — it made good business sense.

The highly ethical nature was only part of the community's culture, which began growing in directions all its own. In keeping with the community's sense of humor, I proclaimed myself *Moderating Dictator*, issuing edicts about FrankelBiz policy and writing the semi-regular newsletters that gave members different views on everything from online chicanery to insider strategies.

The Second Level: From Acceptance to Evangelism

Then something magical happened. We reached a point at which members began to take ownership of the community, participating and furthering creation and expansion of the list. It first manifested itself when someone decided to refer to the members as "FrankelBees." It was a phrase that immediately caught the fancy of all the list members, each one offering the others a "special FrankelBee discount."

The culture took a giant leap forward when I added another clearly branded value: *Frankel's Free Clinic*. Building on the fundamental branding strategy of accessible, straightforward, actionable support, the clinic was actually a one-hour chat session, held every Monday morning, in which

FrankelBees — or potential Bees — could drop in for my business advice free of charge. At least that's how it started. While every clinic began that way, almost every session ended up being more like a real-time solution session, with FrankelBees offering resources and trading tips, often culminating in productive business deals right there on the spot.

I also made it abundantly clear that outside of every Monday morning, the FrankelBees were free to use the chat room for their own purposes whenever they wished.

More community. More value. More responsiveness.

The successful culture spurred membership growth way past 10% per month, with FrankelBees volunteering ideas on how to make the community better and more effective. Some of the ideas were great. Some were pretty bad. But all were an indication of genuine, compelling brand loyalty.

At this point, the only real revenues being generated by the community were those derived from new business leads and referrals, which themselves were not insignificant. After all, that was the point of the list. But very soon it became evident that the momentum of the list — through its added-value programs — were taking it to another level. The group was humming with activity, churning out an average of ten legitimate business propositions a day. Enough to prompt some grouches to complain of over-activity. I interpreted the responsiveness differently. I suspected that we had a branded community who passionately embraced a clearly articulated brand strategy: these people wanted action and understood that their involvement was the driving force behind expansion of the service. Their responsiveness was what convinced me that the list was ready for its second revenue stream: we began to accept advertisers.

Level Three: Turning the Community into Revenue

The FrankelBiz advertising model was a complete departure from regular advertising models. We not only advertised the sponsors' messages in the footers of each message. We created bounty programs for them: FrankelBees that referred accounts to the advertiser got paid commissions on every sale the sponsor closed. The advertisers were blown away by the responsiveness of the list. The FrankelBees were amazed at how much cash - instead of barter or empty promises — arrived in their mailboxes. The key was that this program was based on the central FrankelBiz brand strategy of delivering real benefits, not hype. To the many FrankelBees who had been disappointed in the few cents per month their websites' banners were generating, our checks for hundreds of dollars became a source of inspiration, motivation — and most importantly — continuation of the FrankelBiz brand. It was a resounding success.

All this from what began as a newsletter. With more still to come.

At this point I should mention that my newsletters were becoming less frequent, being published on a monthly basis, and almost always in commentary style. The interactivity of the list became more finely tuned. The ratio of rejected posts was way down, which meant that the FrankelBees — even new ones — were easily absorbing the brand's culture, quickly and efficiently.

There were, however, some land mines to avoid.

Looking out for land mines: protecting interactivity among members

Throughout the first year, I received a lot of suggestions from FrankelBees, mainly concerning new features and services to add to the community — another great signal of brand success. Of all, the most requested feature was for a directory of FrankelBees, listing each one's service and contact information. The notion seemed to make sense. But I rejected it every time. Here's why:

You always have to be careful that your tactics don't interfere with your brand's basic strategy. And sometimes, that means defying conventional wisdom. While a central directory may have seemed to make sense on the surface, it would have destroyed the FrankelBiz concept, because core strength of the FrankelBiz brand lay in the *interactivity* of our membership. In other words, members would have by-passed posting to the list at large in favor of accessing a database of merchants. A move like that would have killed the very force that drove FrankelBiz. Realizing that every piece of FrankelBiz e-mail represented a new hope for new opportunity, I declined the directory concept.

Stepping up a level — empowering the members

By the second year, the brand strategy had been firmly embraced — and evangelized — in the way a successful brand should be. By design, we had spent no money marketing the brand; our growth was totally referral-driven and we had grown our membership into the thousands. Deals were churning. Responsiveness was high.

It was time to take it to the next level.

The essence of the FrankelBiz brand was to do business, not whine about it. But over the first twelve months, I had noticed that the brand attracted a sub-culture of entrepreneurial micro-businesses. These were small — okay, tiny — businesses who believed in the promise of cheap PC's, monthly flat-rate dial-up and do-it-yourself websites. The global access of the web made the web itself an integral part of their business operation. They had the PC's. They had the monthly flat-rate dial-up. And they had the do-it-yourself websites. The two things they didn't have were exposure and marketing budgets.

That was the need we filled with FrankelBiz.com, a web-based solution that allowed anyone (preferably a FrankelBee) to create their own affiliate program amongst other FrankelBees, essentially recruiting a commissioned sales force on a pay-per-sale and pay-per-lead basis. FrankelBiz.com did all the tracking, reporting and billing for participating merchants. We provided online catalogs that displayed their products and services. And we did all that for only $10 a month, plus a tiny slice of the commissions they paid out. Agents were allowed to sign up for free, which meant that except for the $10 monthly fee, this was as good as a pay-if-you-play proposition gets.

The program was also extremely consistent with the brand's other community programs, for example, any FrankelBee who opened a site on FrankelBiz.com could announce that opening to the FrankelBiz list, which in turn encouraged more activity on both.

The main question in the public's mind was why anyone would want to join FrankelBiz.com when there were already turnkey affiliate programs out there. My feeling was — and still is — that none of the other turnkey affiliate programs are branded as effectively as FrankelBiz.com. Our brand is one of straightforward, community-based support.

Because the brand message is so clear, so strong and so effective (Merchants and Agents have to lumber through a similar set of FAQ's before they can participate), I hoped that the small and micro-businesses would choose FrankelBiz.com over those other well-publicized alternatives.

And that's exactly the response we got.

The bad news? The technological partners were unable to deliver the product to our specifications — and FrankelBiz.com failed. The news was received by the community in the only way we could have hoped: with an enormous amount of support and vocal gratitude for trying.

I got more notes of support and inspiration for that failure than almost any other success.

That's a strongly branded community.

The Next Frontier

So what have we really learned from this? Mainly, that on the web or off, brands grow even stronger when you build a branded community around them. The stronger your brand, the more loyalty it commands. When your community accepts your commitment to them, they return the favor by being more responsive.

How much more? Consider this:

In the branded communities with which I've been involved, the minimum response rates from those communities has been ten percent. More often, closer to 25%. Compared that to the fleeting, price-driven 1% to 3% everyone else is resigned to accept. In a branded community, your cost per lead is lower. Your cost per sale is lower. Your repeat purchase rate is higher, as is your margin per sale.

Evangelism: Recruitment and response

The key philosophy behind branded community is fairly simple and revolves around two basic tenets:

1 A user base is actually your greatest sales force.
2. The more you give your community, the more they give back.

The only question is how to motivate that sales force so that they serve both their interests and your own. As you've seen above, motivating the user base — if done properly — will cause your community members to return more often, contribute to the growth of the brand and enrich the results drawn from belonging to the community. Realize from the very beginning that your brand's business — like virtually every other business on the planet — is fundamentally about people, not inventory. You can produce as much inventory as you like, but unless the people are motivated to buy it, there's no business. So emphasize the aspects of the brand that affect the people, rather than "the stuff" you're selling. You'll find that the more human benefits you deliver, the more rapidly your users will embrace and evangelize your brand.

Empowerment as a foundation

One of the strongest human motivators is empowerment, which I define as that which not only makes people feel better about themselves, but delivers a tangible benefit capable of creating real changes in people's lives. Being a cultural haven, your brand has an opportunity of leveraging this concept on several levels.

The main component in most of these programs is drawing the users themselves into the programs, inviting their participation so that they feel an emotional responsibility for the propagation of the program.

You'll also find that as a result of empowering the users and knowing their needs and wants, launching special offers to your Branded Community will result in much higher response rates. This typically occurs because your programs are continually building profiles with increasing accuracy while simultaneously building your constituents' emotional brand loyalty. In effect, the Branded Community responds as much out of its emotional support for a venue it values as it does out of genuine commercial need. People who are interested in the survival of their Branded Community will respond at higher rates to ensure its survival.

Chat functions: Right and wrong

I want to take a brief moment here to issue a warning about chat functions, because it's really a super example of how technology alone is rarely a solution — and can actually cause more grief than it solves.

The first thing that a newbie client suggests to expand his site's brand on-site is usually a chat room. A place where parties drawn to the brand might congregate in real time to ask questions and discuss issues relating to the brand's product or service. At first, it seems like a great idea — and it is.

But only when properly implemented.

A well-done chat room is always manned by a brand representative who can authoritatively answer questions. If not a representative, then at least enough people to convey the perception that the brand really merits a chat room all its own. The well-run chat room becomes a watering hole for brand expansion through user-empowerment. It reinforces your commitment to your customers and often contributes news ideas for your own product development.

On the other hand, nothing trumpets "failure" and "loser" more clearly than a chat room with nobody in it. It is the ultimate experience in loneliness and worse than that, communicates that absolutely nobody feels strongly enough about your brand to even show up to your party. For that reason it is imperative that you always schedule chat events for specific period of time, to be held at specific periods of time. By rigorously holding to your event schedule, members understand the value of the event and make it their business to attend. This results in a higher perceived value for the event.

Conversely, when the event ends on time, the members are left "wanting more" —- which is exactly what you want. It's the surest way to make sure they show up next time.

Those are the little things that complete the branding circle, on the web and everywhere else. It's not so much that you've shown you care as much as the lengths you go to show it.

Community on the site

At this point, it's important to understand the difference between an ordinary site and one that's structured around a branded community. The Branded Community site will foster community growth both strategically and tactically, which means the site's design is as crucial to driving the community's success as any other programs or services you execute.

The typical non-community brands structure themselves along lines of the following chart:

The Overall Brand

E-Commerce/For Profit

Merchandise	Affiliates

The typical e-commerce site is not developed with Branded Community in mind.

As you can see, this scenario precludes any opportunity for community involvement, other than a weak attempt to draw members in through an offer to help the company earn more money for itself by virtue of propping up an Affiliate Program. There is clearly no sense of human involvement here, which is why the vast mjority of sites lack any real sense of community.

A true branded community shifts the perceived emphasis away from the commercial focus of the brand, allowing the more human aspects of the brand to connect with and empower the brand's community members. A true Branded Community resembles something more along the lines of the chart illustrated below. Note how the "Free/Not

For Profit" modules are extremely cost-efficient, yet convey high perceived values.

The true Branded Communitycreates the perception of overshadowing the site's commercial interests.

Site Design, Merchandising and Models

The typical e-commerce site spends way too much time promoting its own commercial interests, which all but destroys any credibility having to do with Branded Community. But even the best sites with killer community programs and services undermine themselves with site design that don't deliver on the promise that Branded Community holds.

As you build the site, design it with Branded Community in mind, carefully balancing your commercial imperatives against the cultural sensitivity that Branded Community requires. Ideally, community members should want to purchase your wares because they are proud to be associated with your brand. If that is not their primary motivation for purchase, then getting them to at least survey your wares should be a lot easier on your site than it would be on a competitor's.

Once they're in, they're in to stay. If there is enough Branded Community product and service in the site, you will find that users will be more forgiving about the volume at which you sales message is set. Your credibility — and sales — will soar.

Finally, avoid using hackneyed terms like "community". These are perceived as blatant attempts to hold hands and sing *Cumbaya* around the camp fire. The term has been so over-used as to mean nothing to anyone, other than a perjorative sneer. Naming your Branded Community, along with each and every one of its components, is a credible and vital method of conveying the cultural and emotional substance of the brand within the service. Applied consistently, this one tool enhances your brand's credibility like no other.

Affiliate Programs

One of the first words out of the mouths of e-commerce owners is "affiliate." For some reason, the uninitiated think that if their affiliate software can just work efficiently, all their marketing problems will be solved. After all, Amazon.com did just fine with the affiliate model.

But as tempting as they are, affiliate programs are not for everyone — you have to fine tune them to your brand. The reason has to do with brand equity more than anything else. While it is true that affilate programs can motivate a certain kind of user base, it's the *way* in which it motivates those users that makes the difference. Affiliate programs that are driven totally by monetary incentives instead of brand qualities, for example, run the risk of destroying the very brand qualities that power your brand's success. The person who's driven by a few extra nickels for every person he or she recruits may not be compatible with your brand's prospects. In fact, when viewed in this perspective,you can see how such a program would actually sabotage the brand by cheapening its image.

Design your affiliate programs around the market for whom they are invented. Where driving profits takes center stage, lead with that. But where the enjoyment of other brand qualitities takes precedence, lead with that and let the profit motive follow. Your brand is your strength.

Graphics online and off

Over and over again, the subject of credibility arises when you build a Branded Community. And since the web is a graphically-driven environment, your choice of graphical styles and subjects are every bit as important as your text-based choices. For that reason, you want to avoid any art that strays from the notion that your brand is wholly original and sincere.

Clip art, cliché art, sub-standard photography and bad illustrations all serve to detract from your brand's credibility. Original styles and graphics will enhance the brand's credibility, if they are balanced between reminiscent tradition and home-grown executions. The more distinctive, the more brand-intensive the site will become.

If executed properly, graphical icons and elements travel well beyond the web site, appearing on merchandise and offline products, sold purely on their brand association and providing ancillary profit centers where none before existed.

Third party endorsements and alliances

Your brand can merchandise its credibility and track record by strategically displaying its associations with legitimizing third parties, especially those with brands that resonate with the Branded Community. To the prospects viewing your brand, this speaks clearly and reassuringly to them in their language. Remember, too, your brand represents an opportunity for other companies to display their identities to the members of your branded community, which can represent serious advertising revenue.

And *don't* explain the whole story.

Realize that every sales piece distributed to the community should be designed to motivate the prospect to *contact you* for more information. That means attaching a link or URL within every communication that invites the member to visit yet another facet of your brand's experience. A very common entrepreneurial mistake is *over-informing* the members. When you over-inform, you give the prospect reasons for *not* contacting you. Give them just enough information to make them want to click through to complete the rest of the story.

Become a central resource.

While the rest of the sector engages in undercutting and commodity-based tactics, your brand needs to develop a program whereby it gives freely to its community. Archives of articles, graphic files and other no-cost items should be available on the web site for free download to the community at large. My own archives contain hundreds of articles on all kinds of branding topics. Some I was already paid for; others were free newsletters that were published on *FrankelBiz*. All of them are available to anyone wishing to find out more about branding on or off the web.

You should do your best to establish those types of resources, as well. And it doesn't have to be on the web. You can do it just as easily with a free "fax-back" system that's driven by a toll-free number, a cheap PC and about $50 of software.

This reinforces your brand's position as the category authority. After all, everyone else in the category jealously guards their data. When the buzz gets around that your brand is an open library (and it will), the brand will take on the altruistic flavor that it inspired.

Pro-actively Creating an Open Environment

Overall, the guiding star of Branded Community is the brand's ability to foster and nurture an open environment, in which community members are encouraged to participate. Simply offering programs and technology will not produce the kind of genuine warmth that propels a community from a simple user base into a pro-active evangelistic sales force.

Your brand must — from the outset — make a point of strongly encouraging its community to take an active role in the direction and development of the brand and its activities. By extending its hand to the community in a genuine, public fashion, and then supporting its offer with tangible actions, the community will come to trust your brand in the manner you wish it to be perceived.

Managing the Branded Community

All of that being said, you must accept the fact that every single interaction between the brand and its community members must be *managed*. Every action, program and service must perform within the ethics and character that is your brand. Just as important as offering and implementing each program and service is their appropriate publicity. No matter how wonderful the Branded Community becomes, you will find that unless you tell your members about it — and tell them often — they simply will not know, remember or understand.

Promoting upcoming events and occasions, reporting on the progress of existing activities, issuing updates and bulletins are all fundamental to creating the perception that the community is a dynamic, thriving, ever-growing entity. Publicizing the dynamics of a Branded Community to its members— when it's properly branded — is never mistaken for spam, but valued as an integral source of information.

Open Management: The Ultimate Goal

The successful Branded Community will evolve to the point where the community itself will take on the appearance of managing the community by itself. When you get to this point, you will witness what I call the Open Management of the Branded Community. This is where community members assume responsibility for the growth of the community, suggesting programs and extensions of their own, forming off-shoot interests of their own.

It's in your brand's best interests to carefully monitor these activities and where appropriate, offer its help in fulfilling the wishes of its community members. Not every idea is a good one, but more than one great product idea has fallen from the lips of a dyed-in-the-wool fan.

If you listen closely and watch carefully, your Branded Community will lead you into new markets and opportunities where buyers await your next branded product — both online and off.

ACTION ITEMS – CHAPTER SEVENTEEN

1. If your brand were personified by one human, who would it be?

2. If your brand were personified by one *employee*, who would it be?

3. If you could create a library in your company, which of your company's papers and books would you allow the public to check out for a week

4. How many people in your company would you allow to meet with the public free of charge every week for an hour

5. Go through your company's past jobs and pull out basic materials that could give prospects a head start on their tasks – which materials would you give them for free?

6. What ancillary subjects interest your prospects the most – besides those of your core business?

7. What could your company do to foster and grow the businesses of its prospects among each other?

18

BRANDING THE SUCCESSFUL ALLIANCE

If there's anything you should be gleaning from this tome, it's that online culture and offline culture are two very different worlds. There are things that work great in offline culture that fall flat on their face when they go online. And there are some concepts that port beautifully from one world to the other. Then there are those that sort of get stuck in between, somewhat Like Jeff Goldblum in *The Fly*. This is about where strategic alliances — *branded alliances* — fall.

Borrowing a little from both worlds, you'll find that branded alliances are really a new breed of tactic. Sure, it sounds an awful lot like the regular old alliance. But if you take a really, really close look, you'll find that the rules have changed.

These days, your alliances have to be more than merely strategic. They have to be branded alliances. And before we get too far, let me explain Frankel's Tenth Law of Big Time Branding:

There is no such thing as co-branding.

Boy, am I going to take heat for that one.

Branding is a leadership issue. It's about differentiation, not blending into the wallpaper. It's about leading, not following. So while it may seem tempting to ally yourself with other companies sporting other brands, keep in mind that there can only be one lead dog pulling the sled.

Your brand.

It's fine to partner with other brands, just don't give them equal billing in your space. For example, if you're selling long distance telephone service and you happen to be reselling AT&T service, it's a huge mistake for you to be "co-branding" with AT&T. By putting their brand up there on the marquis right next to yours, you're essentially under-cutting your value. You're perceived less as being *associated* with them than you are being *reliant* on them.

Real bad look, leadership-wise.

Understand that I'm not saying you can't or shouldn't invite more brands to your party. You can and you should. But let them hold their own, in their own space. So if you're reselling AT&T long distance, sell your brand first — and stress that "we insist on the very best, which is why we only use AT&T. You're happy. They're happy. Everyone wins and your brand is still Numero Uno.

How the Rules Have Changed — and Why

I want to take a minute and explain why the rules have changed so much. If you recall that bit I did about "mass media now becoming media for the masses," you'll understand that one of the crucial components of all marketing today is media. And while media has certainly changed since 1930, it has completely morphed at least three more times since 1960. But even if you added all the prior mutations together, they still wouldn't equal that transformation that modern media has undergone since 1990. The web has completely turned the tables, allowing a mass of individuals global access to an infinite amount of data.

The choice of when, where and how to retrieve that data is now up to each individual's own values and tastes. Which means that for the first time in history, psychographics play an even greater role than do demographics.

Why all the rehash? Because up until this point, I've pretty much constrained my yakking to *your* brand and *your* audience. But now we're about to take our first branded baby steps into the Great Marketing Unknown. We're going to spread our branded wings and see just how high we soar — or how quickly we drop. And both you and I know that we're going to do whatever we can to make our first flight successful. And we're going to do that by hooking into the partners that we think can help us best.

But if we choose those partners according to the wrong criteria, we're going to sink faster than a brick in the shallow end. And that's why I'm rehashing this.

The notion of strategic alliances is nothing new. Basically, it boils down to trading your way around town instead of burning your own cash. Traditionally, that was done through the older media structure. Remember, that back in the Paleolithic era, television and radio and print were hopelessly expensive. The best hope any new brand had for success on a national level was hitching itself to the coattails of an existing national brand, in hopes of gaining national acceptance and distribution. These were strategic alliances, not branded alliances. And they were built like this:

1 **Driven by high awareness:** Most of the time, sponsors pooled their resources and hooked them into television programming. Today's soap operas, for example, began life as sponsored vehicles to sell everything for the modern housewife. In fact, for a while there, the household product giants actually produced the shows they sponsored. Again, it was the strict demographic model at work: lots of housewives tuning in at lunchtime meant lots of housewives watching, learning and memorizing every word from our sponsor. Or, if you prefer, millions of kids mesmerized every Saturday morning by their favorite cartoon show. Same thing.

2 **Product-based alliance:** The giant animals didn't mind carrying the smaller partners, especially when the alliance was compatible in nature. Free tickets to the circus inside every box of Lucky Charms seemed like a win-win proposition, because chances were that the same people who wanted to go to the circus were big Lucky Charms fans, too. More cereal boxes out the door, more fans into the tent, everybody wins.

3 **Shared demographics:** Because the only game in town was mass media, the two partners had to be compatible demographically, as well. There was no way that Lucky Charms would pack a catalog from Victoria's Secret into the box.

4 **Shared media:** Of course, if you were handcuffed into sharing demographics, you were completely manacled to your host's choice of media, as well. Which meant that even if Lucky Charms were to be compatible with your Victoria's Secret catalog, there was absolutely no chance that it would pass muster on Sunday night's rerun of *The Big Valley*.

5 **Distribution based:** Not all fits were controlled by media, however. There was also the nightmare of distribution. Packing your product on to another was a rare but useful tool if every other aspect of the deal — and there were lots of them — matched up perfectly. It was certainly a way to gain distribution into new geographical markets. Shrink-wrapping Oral B toothbrushes to tubes of toothpaste works like that, but not much else does.

When you step away from that model, you begin to see why I call it the Dying Non-Branded Alliance. Oh, it still works for most of Industrial America. But it's becoming less effective as you read this sentence. And the reason it's becoming less effective is because the media has mutated into a free-for-all of individual human choices.

There's no question that the Non-Brand Alliance is circling the drain. The remaining question is, what's taking its place? Very simple: the Branded Alliance.

The reason why the Branded Alliance is coming on so strong is that it's based on — you guessed it — the *branded compatibility* of its partners, rather than their traditional market strengths. It goes something like this:

6 Driven by strong brands: The more the media breaks down, the less clout it has to influence masses in swift, single strokes. The result — at least for Big Time Brands — is the emergence of alliances that are based on the end-users' wants and needs. It doesn't matter when it's *shown* to the end user anymore, because the Branded Alliance partners know that their end users don't rely on that model — end users are seeking out what they want, when they want it. And when they seek it out, the Branded Alliance makes sure to be there for them.

7 Products and services mix compatible brands: If you're old enough to remember the Beatles — or at least the twelve inch vinyl records on which they first recorded — you can also recall the days when the only thing you could find in a coffee shop was food. In those days, the average Denny's or Bob's concerned itself with selling you something to eat along with a usually horrible cup of coffee.

Today, if you walk into a Starbuck's, the only way you can find the coffee is by sniffing your way past the CD's of blues music, the ceramic gift mugs, gourmet lollipops and who knows what else. Why? Because Starbuck's is hip enough to know that the same people who dig blues, ceramic gift mugs and gourmet lollipops are the same types of people who dig their java.

Did someone say *psychographics*?

And yet, some of the big boys still don't get it. When was the last time you saw anything other than food and bad coffee at Denny's?

Interesting, too, how service and product can all get jumbled together with virtually no other commonality than user psychographics. You like computers? You like strong coffee? Bitchen! Let's gene-splice them and call it a cyber-cafe.

8 **Data-intensive:** Whereas the major role of the Dying non-Branded Alliances was simple unit movement, the big prize of Branded Alliances is the sharing of data. As I mentioned before, data is the crude oil of the twenty first century. And psychographic data is about as elusive a creature as you'll find. So if you can track and share information about who loves cheese cake and where they prefer it be delivered, you've got yourself some real value there. It also means you probably don't have to waste all that money on media spillage, because you can target only those psychographics with a high-propensity toward your cheesecakes. That makes your marketing cheaper and more efficient, which makes your brand more profitable.

So if you can see how different the two alliance models are, you can also see how ridiculous it would be to structure your alliance programs with the wrong blueprint. The plain truth is that the fall of mass media is fuelling the importance of brand value. And since branding is so key to individuals' emotions, only those alliances based on Big Time brands will enjoy the maximum benefits of the alliances they create.

It also means that you have think carefully about who your dance partners are.

Avoiding the Unspeakable Dangers

At this point, let me recap the three most important points about creating a Branded Alliance:

1. Start with a strong brand
2. Psychographics over Demographics
3. Avoid the Unspeakable Dangers

The reason I spent as much time as I did on the previous section was to get you to this part, because this is where panic often shoves aside our better business judgments.

Anyone who wants to ally themselves with someone or something else clearly is owning up to the fact that they can't make the trip alone. Oh sure, you can always make the argument that smart alliances allow you to spread your resources around that much further, but let's be honest here: if you had your way, you'd pay your own way and not have to struggle with the hassles and conference calls that alliances bring with them.

Face it. You can't fly this bird alone and you're going to need a co-pilot. But how can you be sure that you're selecting the Red Baron and not Snoopy? You may want to scan this checklist that will help you avoid the unspeakable dangers of alliances:

Efficient is better than big: Everyone always gets excited when Murray the accountant rushes down the hallway, breathlessly announcing that he just got off the phone with MegaPower Industries, who just agreed to the terms sheet of the company's new strategic alliance.

That may be good news. But it may be terrible news, too.

Because the one thing that nobody counts on with big companies is that they are, well, big. And successful at what they do. Which means that things are going along just swimmingly for most of them and that it's not really in their interest to change things all that quickly. Think about it. If you had a job where you finally got things under control, would you be incentivized to radically change things around? Especially when it had absolutely no impact on your pay-check?

Of course not. The folks at Goliath Industries get paid to meet their quotas. And as long as they do, they have no reason to shake things up. They're not entrepreneurial, like you. These are caretakers. People who really like your ideas and want to move ahead and *will definitely take it up with the review committee at the next quarterly strategy session.*

Sure, big companies have big bucks. But what they don't offer is usually what you went to them for in the first place: an agenda. As a rule, the bigger the company, the slower it functions, as your proposals and an action plan slowly oozes through the corporate layers until it dies a slow, drawn-out death, gasping hopelessly on the desk of some middle manager.

You're far better off looking for a company that's in the delivery business. People whose livelihoods depend on getting things done, instead of shoving them into the next in box. Work with people whose sales cycles are measured in days, not months. The people who pride themselves on effi-ciency are the people you want to partner with.

Hungrier is better than popular: As long as we're on the topic of incentivized partners, I'll take hungry businesses over popular ones any day of the week. It's easy to get lulled into a false sense of security by announcing an alliance with a partner whose name is on everyone's lips. But while the puff value can't be dismissed, in terms of action, you want to link up with a team who has a point to prove to the world.

The smart move is to harness the hormone-laden, angry-young-man, gonna-show-the-world-who's-boss energy that fuels the growth of so many new companies. Hitch those animals to your wagon and watch it fly.

Sure, you won't be able to brag as loudly at cocktail parties, but you will be able to grab everyone else's market share.

Monsters have their own agenda: Alright, by now you should be getting the idea that if your partner isn't brand compatible, you could be in for a rude surprise. Perhaps no surprise is any more rude, however, than the Behemoth's Hidden Agenda.

Behemoth's Hidden Agenda occurs when some company, like say, Goliath-Tech approaches you to create a strategic alliance. The mere fact that they approached you should be your first clue that something isn't quite kosher there. After all, when the CEO of Goliath-Tech spends more on his lunch than you do on your monthly mortgage payment, you must know that's something is up.

What's up is almost always a wolf in sheep's clothing, where the lumbering suitor proposes the moon and the stars and fills your overworked brain with visions of untold wealth. The less-sophisticated fall into the money trap, complete with terms, conditions and performance clauses that would make Superman cringe with horror.

The true agenda, of course, is that the monolithic monster really has no intention of ever making the alliance work. In fact, just the opposite: it probably is making the deal to keep your company out of its market. Essentially buying you out of the competitive arena. Lest you think it doesn't happen often, try running a patent search on just about anything you wish. Lots of great ideas have bought their way into obscurity, all in the name of preservation of market share.

Those kinds of mistakes happen far less frequently when you select your allies based on your mutual brand compatibility.

Always brand upward: Choosing the ally that's suitable for you isn't all that difficult, but just to make sure you do the job correctly, try to keep in mind what my aunt always said to her daughter: "It's just as easy to marry a rich man as a poor man."

After sending her daughter to the finest schools and paying rather handsomely for the privilege, she wasn't about to have the kid fall in love with Ernie the tow truck driver. Better she should marry a nice young doctor — or at least a nice boy with a couple of consonants after his name.

Same thing with your strategic partners. It does no good for you to partner with a business whose values, ethics and brand qualities aren't up to yours. Sure, they'll benefit by hooking up with you, but all that work you did on your brand will go straight down the toilet. So while Godiva Chocolates may want to swap vows with Neiman-Marcus, they may want to think twice about returning the affections of 99 Cent Stores.

The worst example of this I ever personally witnessed occurred with a brand of women's jeans that had soared to national popularity seemingly overnight. Although they had enjoyed a terrific run of success, they suddenly found themselves in a cash poor position and needed to liquidate inventory — quick. Seizing upon the opportunity, a mass merchandiser — let's call them J-Mart — offered to buy the whole enchilada from them. Everything from 42 Short to 32 Long. There was only one catch:

J-Mart would only buy the lot if the brand labels were left intact.

The company now had a really tough decision on their hands. They had clawed their way into the minds of almost every American teenage girl. They were found on the shelves of just about every upscale department store throughout the country. In their minds, they had not only built the finest upscale brand for women's jeans, they had built one that was *invincible*.

Or so they thought

Ignoring everyone's advice — which was to sell J-Mart the goods with the brand label torn out — the company shipped the entire lot to J-Mart with the labels intact. Within 24 hours roughly half of the upscale department stores discontinued carrying the brand. By week's end, nearly a decade of work had evaporated. The brand was destroyed. The company filed chapter something.

See what comes from hanging around the wrong kind of people?

Sign a pre-nup before the wedding: Look, I'm as romantic as the next guy, but the previous few points should be enough to teach you that even the best laid plans can end up in court. Although any alliance can implode for unknown reasons, the chance of it happening with a brand-compatible ally are far lower. That's not an accident, either. Because when you ally yourself with a brand-compatible partner, there are other issues besides channels, distribution and unit movement in play. When you bring brands into the mix, you bring the culture, values and ethics that help define those brands. So the chance of anyone faking it are really remote and the chances of success far greater

Nevertheless, things can still happen, which is why I recommend that you always leave each other an out. That way you can both have fun tonight, but still respect each other in the morning if things don't work out.

Seek where you least expect to find them: The hardest habit to break after years of demographic slavery are our own Pavlovian reflexes. Who can blame you? If you're in the software business, it's only natural to think of tech sources for your product. But I always try to hunt for partners where they least expect me to find them.

If I'm marketing an athletic shoe, why not cross-sell it with one of those God-forsaken neon-red athletic drinks?

Is athletic shoes and drinks too obvious? Fine stretch it further — the soundtrack to the Space Jam movie? You start putting all this together and you can see how Warner Brothers, Adidas and Gatorade can find themselves in a store that doesn't necessarily sell athletic gear, but appeals to the person who's consumed by sports. That's not a shoe store. It's not a food store. And it's not a music store.

It's all three — or maybe none at all.

The point is that brand qualities bring products and services together in a psychographic way that we're just not used to. After three generations of demographic drills, we've become accustomed to marching in straight lines and not talking after the bell rings. Those days are over. Which means the pool of potential allies has increased geometrically for you.

You just have to start looking for them where you'd least expect them.

ACTION ITEMS – CHAPTER EIGHTEEN

1. List five reasons why you should joint venture with another brand.

2. List five reasons why you should *not* joint venture with the brands you listed in #1.

3. List five criteria that you seek in a partner that would further your own brand's values and appeal.

4. List five possible candidates that are brand compatible with your company.

5. List five benefits – for each of you – that could result from the joint venture.

6. Prepare a rationale that is a bulletproof argument as to why your brand should take the lead in the joint venture.

19

CREATING THE BIG TIME BRAND

So what have we learned from all this? Well, I'd like to think that perhaps after all this effort, maybe a few more people will understand what branding is and why it's so important. Branding on or off the web goes way beyond the mere commercial world you and I slave in. It's a human thing. A cultural connection to those with whom we interact. Branding is as much a social tool as it is a business tool.

While we've all been taught that charts and ledgers and graphs and numbers are the basis for any rational decision, in the end, people do business with people they like. They stay loyal to those people when they're given the means to articulate that loyalty.

And that's the definition of a Big Time Brand.

Can you create a Big Time Brand? Maybe. But if you admit you can't, you're halfway home. If you still want to try, do what physicians do:

Try it out on someone else.

One of the best exercises I do in seminars in invite everyone in the room to help me brand something that they don't own. It could be a pencil. The light fixture. The fashionable undergarment on the lady in the third row. It doesn't matter. What does matter is that you approach the branding task from a perspective in which you have no interest. The reason for that is simple: it takes you out of the client role and places you where you ought to be, in the role of a prospective end user.

If you really want to have fun, try this out on one of your best friend's businesses and watch them as they suggest strategies for their own businesses. Try to get them to see things from their potential end users' points of view. Most of the time, it won't happen. A few times, your friend may actually get annoyed. But you'll walk away with an accurate demonstration of just how difficult it is to brand yourself.

Don't get me wrong. Some people can and do create their own Big Time Brands. I just haven't covered all of them here. But for the vast majority, I recommend giving it a try, if only to recognize when the next "expert" tries to pull the wool over your eyes. Personally, my theory is to know just enough about something to know when you're about to get screwed.

But I digress.

I think that as long as you keep a copy of Frankel's Laws of Big Time Branding around, you ought to give it a shot. Thinking of yourself as your end users' only solution will train your brain to think less about yourself and more about those end users' problems. Another thing to keep in mind is not to go for the clever stuff right away. I'd much rather be clear than clever, and you should, too. Remember that the most important part of creating a Big Time Brand is articulating it clearly. Once you think you've done that, then you can get cute. But not any time before.

Don't forget that the vast majority of the world's communication was created by committees whose only purpose was to create a message that wouldn't get them fired. With most of the world swamped in a sea of meaningless messages, the clearly focused stand out like sore thumbs. People see them first and remember them the most.

Remember, too, that your market is comprised entirely of human beings. Not personal computers. Not addresses in a database. People, like you and me. And they welcome a friendly mind-linked connection as much as you and I do.

Above all, remain true to your integrity and your belief in your brand. Wear the mantle of leadership with courage and pride, knowing that no one can follow until you take that lead. As an individual or multi-national, the essence of Big Time Branding is taking advantage of a new world of media in which you no longer have to pretend to be all things to all people.

You are rewarded for being yourself. And that's what Big Time Brands are really all about.

APPENDIX A:

FRANKEL'S LAWS OF BIG TIME BRANDING

Frankel's Prime Directive: Branding is not about getting your targets to choose you over your competition. Branding is about getting your prospects to see you as the only solution to their problem.

First Law of Big Time Branding: Brands are not about you. Brands are about them.

Second Law of Big Time Branding: If the branding is wrong, so is everything else.

Third Law of Big Time Branding: Advertising grabs their minds. Branding gets their hearts.

Fourth Law of Big Time Branding: Build from your strengths.

Fifth Law of Big Time Branding: If you can't articulate it, neither can anyone else.

Sixth Law of Big Time Branding: The success of a brand varies directly with the ability to accept the mantle of leadership.

Seventh Law of Big Time Branding: The stronger your brand, the less susceptible you are to pricing issues and competition.

Eighth Law of Big Time Branding: The brand begins in the business plan.

Ninth Law of Big Time Branding: Advertising is not branding. Branding is branding. Advertising *raises the awareness* of the brand you create.

Tenth Law of Big Time Branding: There is no such thing as co-branding.

First Law of Media Hype: Just because you've heard about it doesn't mean it's well-branded. Branding and awareness are not the same thing.

First Law of Web Branding: The more you niche, the better you do.

Second Law of Web Branding: If you don't get them on

the first page, you don't get them at all.

Inverse Theory of Branding: The smaller your budget is, the stronger your brand must be.

Ubiquitous Brand Test: Are we doing it the <COMPANY NAME> way?

The DIY Corollary: Doing it yourself works — for suicide.

APPENDIX B:

MEANINGLESS BRAND TAG LINES

Tagline/Brand Positioning	Company	Meaning
We answer to the world.	International Paper	Ummmm...
Just do it.	Nike	Do *what?*
Rising.	United Airlines	*What's* rising? Does it show?
Let's make things better.	Philips	Let's start with your brand
Is it in you?	Gatorade	Is what in me?
The dot in "dot com"	Sun Microsystems	Huh?
Long live sport	Adidas	None.
Just imagine.	NEC	No idea.
It's time for clarity.	KPMG consulting	How clear is that?
Always.	Coca-Cola	If you say so....

APPENDIX C:

FRANKELBIZ FAQ'S

READ THIS MESSAGE. If you wish to subscribe to FrankelBiz, you MUST REPLY TO THIS MESSAGE. We require you to respond this way in order to keep goofs, freaks and nuts from subscribing you against your will.
If some wackpot has subscribed you against your will, please send an e-mail to FrankelBiz@listserv.robfrankel.com **with the word "UNSUBSCRIBE" in the SUBJECT and accept our apology.**

BY REPLYING, YOU WILL BE SUBSCRIBED TO FRANKELBIZ AND SIMULTANEOUSLY AGREEING TO ALL THE TERMS OUTLINED HEREIN.
If you're smart, you'll save this message somewhere safe. It's got lots of information.
Revision Date: February 1, 1999

The most recent version of this document can always be retrieved by sending mailto:FrankelBiz@listserv.robfrankel.com with a subject message:

Help

or you can view/download a copy at:
http://www.robfrankel.com/frankelbiz/bizfaq.html
This FAQ document was created by Rob Frankel, President of Frankel & Anderson, which is responsible for any errors that it may contain. Please send corrections, additions, deletions or questions mailto:rob@robfrankel.com
Contents.
0. What is FrankelBiz?
1. How do I subscribe to FrankelBiz?
2. How do I unsubscribe from FrankelBiz?
3. Why am I not getting messages?
4. How do I send a message to the list?
5. What are the guidelines for posting on FrankelBiz?
6. Can I advertise on FrankelBiz?
7. Can I post my resume? Can I post a survey?
8. Can I advertise job announcements on FrankelBiz?
9. How do I customize my interactions with FrankelBiz?
10. What is the best way to pose a question/comment/suggestion to the list?
11. FrankelBiz Archives/Frankel's Free ClinicSM

0. What is FrankelBiz?
FrankelBiz is a moderated email business transaction list devoted to establishing a supportive online business community . It is also home to Rob's regularly published newsletter, in which members receive Rob's latest articles and rants free

of charge, along with:

    Rob's reviews and networking of online business, software/hardware and resources

    Discount programs for software/hardware and business resources

    Basic gossip and other professional means of communication

FrankelBiz exists to go beyond the mere discussion of doing business via the internet, to establish a high-level network of ethical associates who may transact business with one another. We are here to do business, instead of whine about it.

In addition to sharing information, list members may enjoy additional benefits, including discounts from participating vendors on products and services offered by our sponsors and participants.

Topics posted on FrankelBiz include the introduction of members, establishment of business relationships, the offering of goods and services, sharing of successful tips and strategies, queries for resources and professional evaluations/advice. Discussions of ethics and practices may be acceptable, but are considered a by-product of the list and not its main focus.

We're here to do business, but we're here to have fun while we do it. That having been said, you should be aware that this is a moderated list, controlled by a benevolent dictator. Although you may get kicked off for any reason, the most prevalent crimes punishable for banishment are: annoying posts, questionable business practices, spamming, flaming, anti-social behavior or anything else that might piss off the list owner or diminish the atmosphere of people doing deals.

To be brutally honest, this list is NOT for beginners, although they are encouraged to join, lurk and learn before posting. Members should be serious about making the internet work for their businesses, rather than educating others about elementary business issues. While a certain amount of education benefits everyone, you should set your educational barometer at the "real world after college" level. Again, this list is NOT academic by nature or design. Posting a TIP on how to do business in a smarter way is as blatantly educational/self-promotional as you'd want to get (see #5).

Remember, too, that Frankel & Anderson provides FrankelBiz as a meeting place for you. Your membership, activity and participation is YOUR responsibility. BY SUBSCRIBING TO FRANKELBIZ, YOU HOLD HARMLESS ROB FRANKEL, FRANKEL & ANDERSON, INC., AND ANY OF EITHER'S STAFF, ASSOCIATES OR EMPLOYEES FROM ANY LIABILITY WHAT-SOEVER, IN ANY AND ALL MATTERS.

This is an on-line country club where we schmooze and talk and help each other make deals. List membership should be considered something like a Badge of Honor — pinned on your lapel by Groucho Marx.

This is a Private List, meaning that no members' names or e-mail addresses are available for review or analysis by remote command. The membership list of

FrankelBiz is considered the property of Rob Frankel/Frankel & Anderson and not available for public scrutiny or exploitation other than "embedded ads" which may support the list (see below).

Rob Frankel/Frankel & Anderson exclusively owns and retains the right to publish and re-publish any part or all of the content found on FrankelBiz. No other party may re-publish any content found on FrankelBiz without the express written consent of the list owner.

FrankelBiz is owned by Frankel & Anderson, a California corporation. It is operated by Rob Frankel. He can be reached at rob@robfrankel.com or by phone via 818-990-8623. Please direct any administrative or technical questions to rob@robfrankel.com.

1. How do I subscribe to FrankelBiz?

The best way to subscribe to FrankelBiz is to use the Subscription Form at http://www.robfrankel.com/frankelbiz/form.html. Fill out the form completely (which is important if you want to get good solid business contacts) and hit the Submit button.

Save the subscription confirmation from the List Server software in an email folder. Once again, if you wish to be subscribed to FrankelBiz, you MUST REPLY TO THE CONFIRMATION MESSAGE that arrives after submitting your Subscription Form. We require you to respond this way in order to keep goofs, freaks and nuts from subscribing you against your will.

2. How do I unsubscribe from FrankelBiz?

To leave the list at any time send a message to the server, you can either follow the directions found at the bottom of each post, or mailto:FrankelBiz@listserv.robfrankel.com. The SUBJECT of message should say:

UNSUBSCRIBE

If you have a problem, send email to rob@robfrankel.com.

3. I am not getting messages, how come?

The list administrators are ruthless in unsubscribing anyone if there is a "mailbox full," "user unknown", "host unknown" or any other mechanical/internet error. The machine tries a number of times, and if it fails, it removes anyone whose mail is undeliverable. Normal transmission problems and delays will not cause you to be unsubscribed. The server will attempt to deliver mail to each user for up to 5 days, so an intermittent system problem should not cause you to lose messages or be unsubscribed.

If you want to see the latest postings, go to http://www.robfrankel.com/frankelbiz and follow the path to the FrankelBiz archive.

To determine if you are subscribed, simply send a "subscribe" message to FrankelBiz@listserv.robfrankel.com (see item 2. above). If you get back an error saying "already a member" then you know the problem is somewhere on the net, contact your provider. If you get back the "welcome FAQ" it means you had been removed and are now resubscribed.

Habitual offenders may be barred from resubscribing. If you feel that is your case, and you have been unjustly cast out into the ether, you may always plead your case for reinstatement to rob@robfrankel.com.

4. How do I send and reply to messages on the list?

To send a message to everyone on FrankelBiz, mailto:FrankelBiz@listserv.robfrankel.com

If you are replying to a previous message, know that you should only send your email to the individual who originally sent the note. You should investigate the behavior of your email software by looking at what address is produced for the From: field. If the list address doesn't appear there you may type in the list address by hand, or possibly get your software to supply it by using a "Reply to All" command or icon, or a "Group Reply" function.

When you do reply, it's preferable that you cite the post to which you are responding so that the recipient can follow along.

5. What are the guidelines for posting to FrankelBiz?

The best way to make this list work for you is by sharing the stuff that makes you and other list members successful at doing business on the internet, preferably with each other. That means sharing leads, ideas and opportunities with other members in the group.

Where possible, use a clear identifying tag in your subject line of your post. For example, if you're an exporter, and you know a smart way to save money on freight forwarding, your initial post might read "TIP: Bribe customs agents in dollars, not yen". Your post will help others on the list and will show off your expertise in a credible, friendly manner. TIPS can be about any business or marketing-related manner. The more you post, the better — for you and the list.

List member are STRONGLY encouraged to share their FrankelBiz business success stories with the list. By posting your successful experiences with other list members to the list (with a tag like "THANKS, BETTY: Found three-toed sloth" or "RESULTS: Got a new computer cheap!"), you encourage other list members to come forward and participate. This is the purpose of FrankelBiz.

The following Dictator's Edict spells out the revised Acceptable Post policy for FrankelBiz, so please read it carefully:

Every post begins in the Moderator's Dungeon. If, after being flogged, it still passes the test, it makes it on to the FrankelBiz list. In order to make it on to FrankelBiz, its content must meet the following criteria:

A. Provide an opportunity for legitimately expanding business to network and build our web-connected businesses. That means you are seeking help from others with a business need you have. These messages should be preceded by "HELP" or "NEED" in the Subject header of the post.

B. Provide a solution for list members that you believe may be helpful. That means you have a product/service/ability that you believe can further the businesses of others on the list. It does NOT include self-serving messages that do NOT further the business interests of other FrankelBees. So for example, if you represent a shipping company and can get us all really cheap rates on Federal Express, we want to hear about it. But if you simply are looking to sell more bottles of Earthworm Droppings, you're out of luck, doomed to fester on the floor of the Dungeon with all the other rejected posts.

I recommend including a value-add or a discount offer to the list, but if you do, please make it meaningful and exclusive to the FrankelBees. None of this "Free air with every order" crap. I'd rather have NO offer and a compelling post than puffery.

C. Special Cases: As I always say, "Life is a marketing problem." Not everything in life falls neatly into place according to plan. So there are some exceptions to the rules. Say, for example, that it's gift giving season and Earthworm Droppings are very popular gifts to give clients. In that case, you are providing a true service, because you are positioning your product/service/ability as a method of promoting others' businesses.

Personal attacks, disparaging remarks or flames are not allowed on FrankelBiz — unless they're REALLY FUNNY. That's the risk you take. So as the big guy says, "Don't be a schmuck." Stay cool and try to do business. A certain amount of emotion is acceptable, but an annoying, petty attitude can get you booted off FrankelBiz.

Incidentally, THERE ARE NO WARNINGS. A "gentle reminder" nudging at your email in box may appear, but list members are advised that death to the offender on FrankelBiz is swift and unannounced, and that the list owner is not obliged to fire off any kind of notification of impending doom. Like you would in any club, if you have an issue with any one member, take it outside, or in this case, off-list. E-mail the person directly so the rest of us don't have to put up with you.

This is NOT a forum for Multi-Level Marketing operations, Get Rich Quick schemes, MAKE-MONEY-WHILE-YOU-SLEEP quackery or any other enterprise that the list owner may, at his own discretion, deem dubious, unethical, illegal or just plain stupid.

DON'T use the list address to signoff. If someone does this, ignore them. The list owner will take care of them.

DON'T send one-on-one conversations to the list. If the subject only concerns you and one or two intended recipients, send your email to your targets directly. This will generally require that you type in their address and not use your email 'reply' function.

DO include your name and email address at the bottom of all messages to the list. Some mail systems don't include it in the headers AND FrankelBiz DOES NOT ACCEPT UNSIGNED OR ANONYMOUS POSTS. All posts must include he name of the real, live human being posting.

6. Can I advertise on FrankelBiz?

For members, the answer here is a limited yes, but only if your product or service relates to offering a business opportunity. If you do advertise, include the key word "AD:" on your subject line. You may also tag a header with "INTRO:" to introduce yourself and your company, or "UPDATE:" to let people know about an important development, but keep it within reason. Excessive use can really tick members off.

Your best bet for success on FrankelBiz is offering business opportunity as well as fulfilling them. If you offer business, someone else is bound to offer some to you.

If you feel the readers of FrankelBiz would benefit from an informative message you may do so, but keep it very short. Include contact information for interested readers.

The list owner reserves the sole right to embed a list sponsor's ad(s) in the header/footer of each post broadcast by FrankelBiz.

If you object to ads you see on FrankelBiz, please respond directly to the poster, not to the whole list.

7. Can I post my resume or a survey?

The answer is "yes" for resumes, but only if you are an individual seeking employment for yourself. When you post your resume, include the keyword "RESUME:[position title]" on your subject line. For example:

Subject: "RESUME: Brand Manager"

Also include contact information in the body of the E-mail message for interested readers. Employment agencies and other third party postings are not allowed.

Surveys are not allowed on FrankelBiz, with the exception of those administered by the list owner.

8. Can I advertise job announcements on FrankelBiz?

The answer is "yes," but only if your firm is the hiring company, or if you're helping another individual out. Recruiters and employment agencies DO NOT fall into this category and are not permitted to peddle their flesh. If you have any questions, contact the list manager at rob@robfrankel.com.

When you post your job announcement, include the keyword "JOB: [position title]" on your subject line. For example:

Subject: "JOB: Product Manager"

Include contact information in the body of the E-mail for interested readers.

9. What other list server commands will customize my subscription?

To learn more about managing your subscription, send the one line message

help

to the server address: FrankelBiz@listserv.robfrankel.com

One can subscribe to the list in digest form which means that you only receive one message when the amount of list traffic reaches 50000 characters or after 24-hours have passed.

The digest form is useful when you do not post to the list very often.

Send email to FrankelBiz@listserv.robfrankel.com with the message

Digest on

To return to normal mail, use the command

Digest off

If you receive the list in digest form, note that replying to a message will require that you change the outgoing "Subject:" field for the message. Also note that if you quote a previous message, be careful to attribute the quote to its correct author.

10. What is the best way to pose a question/comment/suggestion to the list?

(1) Start by describing your business opportunity/situation. Tell the readers of FrankelBiz how you fit in to the opportunity and describe the need you are trying to fill.

(2) Describe the market factors, potential upside and downside. DON'T EXAG-GERATE YOUR CLAIMS. We're all pro's here and can smell road apples from three miles out.

(3) Tell the list about your background and why you think your proposition is such a good one. If you have a need to be filled, ask the list for solutions, suggestions or leads. If someone helps you out, consider cutting them in on some part of the transaction. After all, this is business and you're entitled to it.

(4) If you need a connection to a person, industry, come right out and ask for it. Just be sure to explain fully why and what you need the connection for.

(5) If you're posting a TIP, explain how your solution is a smarter, more efficient method than usual. Mentioning the potential disastrous consequences of alternative methods, or telling your own experiences are helpful illustrations and boost your credibility.

Remember that no one on FrankelBiz owes you anything. All participation is voluntary. Make your request entertaining rather than demanding.

11. Archives/Frankel's Free Clinic

The FrankelBiz archive may be found at http://www.robfrankel.com/list-archives

Frankel's Free Clinic is a chat session held every Monday morning, from 9 AM to 10 AM Pacific Time at http://www.robfrankel.com/chat/chat.html . This is where Rob donates one hour of free consultation and where other FrankelBees join in and often make new business deals. You can view transcripts of past clinics at http://www.robfrankel.com/frankelbiz/freeclinic .

Rob Frankel, Big Time Branding SM http://www.robfrankel.com

ABOUT ROB FRANKEL

Rob Frankel may be the most widely read on (and off) line branding expert on the planet. In fact, his articles have been translated into many different languages appearing on six different continents and all over the web.

Rob's a branding specialist. Which means he knows how to get the public to like your stuff, and more importantly, buy your stuff. Again and again. On the web or anyplace else, for that matter. Rob's clients include multinational businesses, Hollywood celebrities and even a nonprofit or two.

Unlike traditional branding theorists, Rob Frankel believes that *"Branding is not about getting your prospects to choose you over your competition; it's about getting your prospects to see you as the only solution. to their problem"*

Rob does consulting and speaking gigs. Mainly to companies who sink zillions of dollars into a website or a business and then scratch their heads wondering why it just sits there like a lox.

In addition to speaking and consulting, Rob Frankel has written as Business Opinion columnist for Ziff-Davis' *Internet Business* magazine and is the Moderating Dictator of *FrankelBiz*, the web's first and only transactional list where people do business instead of simply whine about it.

Rob lives and works on a sprawling estate located at *http://www.robfrankel.com*

Rob Frankel emerged from the University of California at Berkeley with a degree in Economic History, a major that Rob invented and contributed to the official sanction of the major at that institution. After serving eight years hard labor at some of the world's largest advertising agencies (Foote, Cone & Belding, DMB&B, etc.), Rob escaped to form Frankel & Anderson, home of Advertising, Marketing & Killer Creative™. Soon after, Frankel &Anderson became America's first totally digital/online agency, expanding its client base worldwide. Today, Rob Frankel consults to all on-line and off-line clients throughout the world.

Rob is the inventor of U.S. Patent #4,264,499, "Foto Pheet" — world's smallest, most portable stand for 35mm cameras. His first book, *The Gentleman's Real Guide to College*, was hailed by *Playboy* magazine as required reading for all college students.

ORDER FORM

This book may not be readily available for purchase in book stores. You may order additional copies of *The Revenge of Brand X* alternatively:

ON THE WEB:

http://www.robfrankel.com and http://www.revengeofbrandx.com
Simply follow the links to the order form. Have a credit card ready. You may also check online bookstores (*i.e., amazon.com, barnesandnoble.com, etc.*) by searching the title.

E-MAIL:

Send to: BrandX@robfrankel.com and include the information below.

First Name: _____

Last Name: _____

Company: _____

Address _____

Address _____

City: _____

State: _____

Zip _____

Phone: _____

Fax _____

E-Mail _____